MUSEUM DIPLOMACY

A VOLUME IN THE SERIES

Public History in Historical Perspective

EDITED BY

Marla R. Miller

MUSEUM DIPLOMACY

TRANSNATIONAL PUBLIC HISTORY AND THE U.S. DEPARTMENT OF STATE

RICHARD J. W. HARKER

UNIVERSITY OF MASSACHUSETTS PRESS
Amherst and Boston

Printed in the United States of America

ISBN 978-1-62534-493-9 (paper); 492-2 (hardcover)

Designed by Deste Roosa
Set in Minion Pro
Printed by Books International, Inc.

Cover design by Frank Gutbrod
Cover photo by Gerd Altmann/Pixabay

Library of Congress Cataloging-in-Publication Data
Names: Harker, Richard J. W., author.
Title: Museum diplomacy : transnational public history and the U.S. Department of State / Richard J. W. Harker.
Description: Amherst : University of Massachusetts Press, 2020. | Series: Public history in historical perspective | "State Department Museums" : The Convergence and Divergence of Public Diplomacy and Public History — "Afghan on top and American on the Bottom" : Exploring Minority identity through dialogue with "war-torn Afghanistan" — Beyond an "Imperialist Undertaking" : Negotiating Transnational Public History Pedagogy — Activating Sites of Conscience Addressing Shared Silences within Parallel (Public) Histories. | Includes bibliographical references and index.
Identifiers: LCCN 2019044477 | ISBN 9781625344922 (hardcover) | ISBN 9781625344939 (paperback) | ISBN 9781613767382 (ebook) | ISBN 9781613767399 (ebook)
Subjects: LCSH: Museum cooperation—International cooperation. | Public history—International cooperation. | United States. Department of State—Museums. | International Partnership Among Museums. | Cultural diplomacy—United States—History—21st century. | Cultural diplomacy.
Classification: LCC AM7 .H37 2020 | DDC 069/.5—dc23
LC record available at https://lccn.loc.gov/2019044477

British Library Cataloguing-in-Publication Data
A catalog record for this book is available from the British Library.

Portions of chapter 3 were previously published in "Museums Connect: Teaching Public History through Transnational Museum Partnerships," *Public History Review* 22 (2015): 56–68.

For Sue

CONTENTS

PREFACE

In the spring of 2011, when I was offered a job at the Museum of History and Holocaust Education (MHHE) at Kennesaw State University (KSU) in Georgia, I was introduced to the Museums Connect program. After accepting the job, I was sent information about the Museums and Community Collaborations Abroad grant (as it was then called), which the Kennesaw museum and the Ben M'sik Community Museum in Casablanca, Morocco, had just been awarded. Thus, as I began my career in museums and public history and started to learn and adapt to the local and regional contexts that shaped my new job, I found myself also working as a project facilitator for this year-long, shared grant between the two museums.

The prospect of working in an international context and traveling to Morocco was exciting. However, I also had questions about the work. Why would a Holocaust and World War II museum work on a project about Islam? What does it mean for American museums and museum professionals to engage in what I later discovered was called "soft power"? These questions mostly remained dormant, overshadowed by the thrill of traveling to Morocco and the pressure of navigating the complexities of international work, all while completing the day-to-day tasks of a new job.

One of the most memorable experiences of the project was my trip to Casablanca. Jet-lagged and facing a week of exhibition development meetings and sightseeing excursions, I, along with my colleague Julia Brock and a team of KSU students, sat around tables with Moroccan students and staff from the Ben M'sik Community Museum and engaged in our first brainstorming session. As we discussed what to include in an online exhibition, the ultimate goal of the project, I was energized by the passion of our Moroccan counterparts, who spoke about their desire to dispel stereotypes of Muslims as terrorists and to address various misconceptions, such as the wearing of hijabs in Morocco. Our students were talking, we were listening, and I was furiously taking notes. As the project developed, the Moroccan group visited the United States, and we conducted Skype workshops, shared blog posts, and exchanged emails. But as the exhibition's development moved from preliminary conversations and workshops to actual decision-making, our Moroccan colleagues' initial ideas were excluded from the final product. Our early brainstorming about forthrightly addressing stereotypes and misconceptions was absent from later discussions. Although I did not realize it at the time, the U.S. partners had created a space for dialogue but did not cede control of the structure or implications of these activities. Ultimately, decisions about the exhibition's form and content remained in our hands as the grant's lead museum, staffed by public history and museum professionals educated and trained in the American professional practices that underpin the Museums Connect program—which itself is administered by the American Alliance of Museums and sponsored by the U.S. Department of State.

These silences and power dynamics were not obvious in the moment, for at the time we were overtaken by our desire to finish the project. Yet on reflection, I see that an initial unease, occasionally manifested in conversations with colleagues, mirrored the larger dynamics of the projects between the two museums. This became clear to me only as I was working on this book, which is a direct response to my experience with Museums Connect. As I broadened the scope of inquiry, my questions, assumptions, thoughts, and ideas increased. This study is my continuing attempt to wrestle with those questions and my experiences.

ACKNOWLEDGMENTS

Writing this book has truly been a shared endeavor, and I am grateful to the many people who supported and helped me throughout. Without the tireless encouragement of Kate Wilson, this book would not have been possible. Since the project's inception, I have been indebted to her good humor, reassurance, prodding, and thoughtful guidance. Likewise, Jeffrey Trask and Alex Cummings have offered advice, commentary, and support. I also owe a deep debt to Carolyn Biltoft and Denis Gainty of the Georgia State University History Department, who were encouraging throughout the process.

During my time as a graduate student at Georgia State University, Cliff Kuhn was one of my biggest supporters. His guidance and passion immeasurably influenced both me and this project. Cliff's guidance made this book better in its earliest days, and he was the epitome of the kind of public historian that I strive to be. I miss him dearly.

Many colleagues and friends deserve thanks. My writing buddy and good friend Ryan Prechter, my partner-in-public-history Sara Patanaude, my dear friend Mark Honnen, and my copyeditor Rachel Berry kept me going with their love, support, and friendly critiques. I sincerely appreciate their help.

I also owe deep gratitude to three scholars whose work, during my early studies, so deeply influenced me that I cannot help but see it shine through in these pages. Justin Willis and Cherry Leonardi at Durham University guided and mentored me as I worked toward my master's degree and introduced me to the plight of the subaltern. Bernhard Struck at the University of St. Andrews introduced a seemingly radical idea—transnational history—to a young undergraduate and has since then never wavered in his support of my academic career.

I've relied on the kindness of strangers across the globe. Museum professionals at various institutions around the world, State Department officials, and staff at the American Alliance of Museums took the time to help an absolute stranger, and without them this book would never have been possible. Many responded with kindness and gave me hours of their time as well as connections and documents, even when I contacted them out of the blue. My debt of thanks is greater than words can express. In particular, I thank Heather Berry, Brooke Leonard, and Madeline Vadkerty of the American Alliance of Museums; Karen (Lea) Perez, Mary Jeffers, and Laura Tedesco at the State Department; and Sally Roesch Wagner and International Partnership among Museums (IPAM) participants Carey Rote, Mark Heppner, and Patoo Cusripituck.

In Birmingham, Johannesburg, Atlanta, Kennesaw, Philadelphia, and Kabul, I have met—in person, via email, over the phone—a myriad of dedicated and thoughtful museum professionals, teachers, students, and community activists who shared their experiences with Museums Connect, read and commented on drafts of my work, and formed the backbone of this study. Hugh Allen, Jeff Stern, Sayeh Hormozi, Lauren Cristella, Nasim Fekrat, Aziz Royesh, Omara Khan Massoudi, and students from Philadelphia and Afghanistan were incredibly gracious with their help. I also thank Lisa Helling and Zalmai Attapoor, of the U.S. Embassy in Kabul, and Fahim Rahimi, director of the National Museum of Afghanistan, for their helpful liaison work.

In Birmingham and Johannesburg I had the honor of speaking to a group of students and professionals whose dedication to eradicating prejudice and making their communities stronger is remarkable. Their time and contributions were incredibly generous. I would be remiss if I did not give Laura Anderson a special word of thanks for all of her help in facilitating my conversations with her colleagues on both sides of the ocean and for her lengthy reflections on her experiences.

Samir El Azhar's friendship throughout our work together as well as his willingness to confront difficult issues of power and engage in an honest and open discussion about his experiences with Museums Connect has had a profound impact on me and this book.

Many people have read and offered comments about this project at various stages of the writing process, both as a dissertation and as a book manuscript. Na Li's advice about parts of chapter 3 facilitated their publication in the *Public History Review.* Her guidance, along with comments from peer reviewers and the journal's editors, helped make that chapter better. The audiences at the 2013 Emory University Graduate Students Conference, the 2014 meeting of the Association of Historians at Georgia State University, and the 2015 meeting of the Southern American Studies Association all contributed to my thoughts about my research. Colleagues and friends who joined Na Li and me to discuss transnational and international public history at the 2017 meeting of the National Council on Public History also deserve special mention, especially Mark Barron, Nan Kim, Ann McCleary, Mattea Sanders, Cameron Walpole, Serge Noiret, and Thomas Cauvin.

My colleagues and friends at the MHHE and at Historic Oakland Foundation consistently remind me to merge theory with practice and to remember that, when a school bus carrying a hundred fifth graders shows up or a thousand people visit a Halloween tour, all bets are off. Along with being a fantastic travel companion in Morocco in 2011, Julia Brock has read countless drafts of my work and been a valuable friend and guide since our early days in Kennesaw. Similarly, Jennifer Dickey has been a constant supporter, proofreader, and friend. Without her friendship, pep talks, and good humor I would not have finished this book. Words cannot do justice to her friendship and her contributions.

I am indebted to the talented and meticulous staff at the University of Massachusetts Press, especially Matt Becker, whose time, advice, support, and guidance have been indispensable. Marla Miller, the editor of the Public History in Historical Perspective series, offered guidance and a keen editorial gaze that has made this work significantly stronger. I am also grateful to the anonymous peer reviewers, whose comments and rigorous edits also made this book better.

I spent many a childhood family holiday driving around the British countryside, visiting ruined cathedrals, castles, and visitor centers, and this triggered my deep love of history, museums, and historic sites. For this I thank my parents, Barbara and Graham Harker. I am deeply grateful for the love and support of our ever-expanding family: Trish, Chris, Poppy, and Betsy Turner; Lucy, Tom, and Emma Hemming; and

Sonya Sharma. My brother, Chris Harker, has read almost everything substantial I've ever written, including this book, and without his help I would never have gotten to this place.

Without the love, support, and unending patience of my wife, Sue, this book would not exist. Sue lived and breathed Museums Connect with me since the beginning, and her patient willingness to listen to me think out loud, to read this manuscript, and to deal with this addition to our lives was remarkable. I dedicate the book to her with my deepest love. I miss her terribly.

ABBREVIATIONS

AAM	American Alliance of Museums, formerly American Association of Museums
BCRI	Birmingham Civil Rights Institute, Birmingham, Alabama
BMCM	Ben M'sik Community Museum, Casablanca, Morocco
CIA	Central Intelligence Agency
DOS	U.S. Department of State
DOS ECA	U.S. Department of State, Bureau of Educational and Cultural Affairs
FRAME	French Regional and American Museum Exchange
IFPH-FIH	International Federation for Public History–*Fédération Internationale pour l'Histoire Publique*
IPAM	International Partnership among Museums
KSU	Kennesaw State University, Kennesaw, Georgia
MCCA	Museums and Community Collaborations Abroad, Museums Connect's name in 2008–11
MHHE	Museum of History and Holocaust Education at Kennesaw State University, Kennesaw, Georgia
NCC	National Constitution Center, Philadelphia, Pennsylvania
NCPH	National Council on Public History
NMA	National Museum of Afghanistan, Kabul, Afghanistan
UNESCO	United Nations Educational, Scientific, and Cultural Organization
USIA	U.S. Information Agency

NOTE ON QUOTATIONS

All interviewees and respondents quoted in this manuscript consented to have their recollections of Museums Connect be published. However, some of the participants in projects between U.S. museums and those in South Africa and Afghanistan were minors. To protect these students, I have given them pseudonyms, even though they shared their reactions and gave consent after they became adults. Where participants' quotations or recollections are drawn from a published source or are publicly available elsewhere, I use their real names. In the case of the project involving the Ben M'sik Community Museum, all participating students were either undergraduate or graduate students, and their real names are thus included. When I use a pseudonym, I place the name inside quotation marks in the accompanying note.

MUSEUM DIPLOMACY

INTRODUCTION

The field of public history is experiencing an international turn. Since the beginning of the twenty-first century, the establishment of academic public history programs across the globe, an increase in the amount of international and transnational public history programming, the rise of public history scholarship situated outside of the United States, combined with the recognition and engagement of U.S.-based scholars and practitioners has resulted in the development of a transnational and global field of public history. Enhanced by the increasing ease of communication, precipitating the faster sharing and debating of ideas and practices, this new mode of considering how the public engages with the past and the role that historians play in this work complements and works alongside national, regional, and local contexts and practices that previously were the only framework for practicing and studying public history.[1]

This international turn has potentially significant consequences and is particularly important in the United States, where the term *public history* originated and the academic discipline codified. The addition of international perspectives, practices, and voices is challenging the pervasive U.S.-centric understanding of the field and the subsequent erasure of international contexts, practices, and scholarship from discussions and analyses of public history as both an academic and practical discipline. By combining transnational and international approaches with local, regional, and national approaches, public historians have a new lens through which to consider the complex nature of working with the public in the creation and presentation of the past. Considering international and transnational perspectives alongside local, regional, and national contexts presents a tantalizing opportunity for U.S.-based public historians to reconsider foundational assumptions, theories, and practices that hitherto have only been considered, tested, or understood in a local, regional, or national context. In so doing, the theory and practice of public history as written and practiced in the United States can become more nuanced and understandable as it relates to practices occurring across the globe.

As a project of the U.S. Department of State (DOS) and the American Alliance of Museums (AAM), the Museums Connect program's international scale and reach, combined with its grounding in U.S. theory and practice and its public diplomacy goals, have made it an important part of this international turn. Because it is rooted in U.S. museum theory, Museums Connect reveals the theoretical and practical issues that emerge from the internationalization of the field of public history, the creation of new international and transnational practices, and the consequent implications for U.S. domestic public history. During the program's ten years of operation (2008–17), participating museums engaged in transnational museum-community collaborations and were thus actors in state-sponsored public diplomacy efforts. During Museum Connect's year-long projects, primarily funded by DOS and administered by AAM, museums in the United States partnered with non-U.S. museums and their communities on collaborative projects. The range and scope of these projects were as diverse as the partnering museums were—including transatlantic dialogues around immigration between museums and their communities in Belgium, Italy, and New York City; an exploration of the legacies of nuclear weapon testing for communities in Kazakhstan and Nevada; and the study of connections between the histories and violent experiences of Chicago and Cambodia.

Public history focuses on the theory and practice of doing history by, with, and for the public. Since the discipline emerged in the United States in the 1970s, rapid technological changes connecting individuals and institutions in real-time communication and collaboration, as well as the gradual shift in global hegemony since the end of the Cold War, have challenged U.S.-based practitioners to consider a broader understanding of the field. Early in the twenty-first century, the emergence of global academic journals, national and international conferences, and a shift in scholarship focus to include non-U.S. perspectives and practices has led U.S. practitioners and scholars to recognize that public history, whether or not conducted by those who call themselves public historians, has been practiced, reflected upon, and analyzed in monographs, journals, and conversations, in diverse national and domestic contexts, for hundreds of years.[2] As public historians and museum professionals around the world have moved beyond international traveling exhibitions and exchanges of scholarship to collaborate across nation-state borders and connect local and domestic issues across the globe, public history has begun to emerge in an international context outside of the United States.[3] A recent abundance of scholarship, perspectives, and reflections on public history practice in countries outside of the United States has caught up with this reality. These developments—often broadly and inexactly termed *international public history*—have had the effect of decentering the United States and shifting the terms of analysis beyond a strict focus on the local, regional, and national. They have also provided a new "glocal" lens through which to consider history making, where international and transnational contexts are placed alongside the local and regional to provide a new geographical mode of analysis that is distinct, and potentially revealing, in ways that are very different from the view through a local or international lens alone.[4]

This shift has led public historians into a rich subfield of practice and study with new questions, considerations, and avenues of study emerging alongside organizations, programs, and practices that broaden the analytical scope of the field. Much of this new work—whether in formal articles, conference proceedings, or website metadata—embraces the term *international*, an umbrella label including public history practiced within the boundaries of the nation-state and assessed with comparative local, regional, and national examples as well as transnational processes of exchange and flow across nation-state boundaries.[5] At the forefront of this work is the United Nations Educational, Science, and Cultural Organization (UNESCO), which was created after World War II and has expanded the geographic lens of historic preservation and internationalized efforts to save endangered cultural heritages.[6] More recently, in 2011, the International Federation for Public History–*Fédération Internationale pour l'Histoire Publique* (IFPH-FIHP) was founded "to create international linkages between public historians and promote the development of a world-wide network of Public History practitioners. The federation's purpose is to encourage, promote, and coordinate, at an international level, contacts, teaching and research in public history."[7] In addition to IFPH-FIHP's network of individual scholars and practitioners, the International Coalition of Sites of Conscience (ICSC), created in 1999, creates a network of sites of historic traumas across the globe to "connect past struggles to today's movements for human rights."[8] The growth of these institutions within a wider international context has influenced U.S. domestic museum practice. "International public history is attracting increasing attention within the wider [U.S.] discipline of public history," declared William Willingham in 2015. "Attendance at the annual meetings of the National Council on Public History (NCPH) now includes historians from a variety of nations, and the meetings contain increasing numbers of sessions devoted to various aspects of public historical practice from an international perspective."[9] At the highest levels of the museum field, the American Alliance of Museums' (AAM) 2016–20 strategic plan stated the organization's belief "[i]n active participation in the global community and embracing international perspectives" and set out to embrace "Global Thinking" with the goal of "connect[ing] US museums to the international community."[10]

The international turn and its effects on domestic, local, and regional U.S. public history practices emerges in distinct ways through this book's analysis of Museums Connect. This well-funded DOS program served the dual role of fostering people-to-people public diplomacy—"the art of communicating with foreign publics to influence international perceptions, attitudes and policies"—and building museum-community collaborations in an international context.[11] Museums Connect projects were transnational in nature: transcending nation-state borders and reflecting the centrality of interconnectedness, exchange, and multiplicity. New products were created in the physical and intellectual spaces between the museums and between the museums and their communities and included numerous agencies on all sides of the partnerships.[12] In studying a program of this geographical and financial scale, this book provides the first in-depth critical analysis of Museums Connect. It argues that we discern new and distinct methods of transnational public history practice by studying these collaborations and that, in tracing the U.S. context and origins of the program, we are able to shine a new light and raise new questions about the central ideas underpinning museum-community collaboration developed in a U.S. national context.[13]

AT THE INTERSECTION OF PUBLIC HISTORY AND PUBLIC DIPLOMACY

Museums Connect stands at the intersection of public history and public diplomacy and in so doing represents a new kind of transnational public history.[14] With its origins in the United States, Museums Connect grew out of changes in U.S. museums and grant making in the twenty-first century. Between 1980 and 2007, the American Association of Museums (AAM changed its name to the American Alliance of Museums in 2012) partnered with the DOS to operate the International Partnership among Museums (IPAM). This robust program connected U.S.-based museum professionals with counterparts in other countries, with the goal of sharing best practices and engaging in individual cultural diplomacy. As Erik Ledbetter, then senior manager of international programs at AAM recalled in a 2007 interview, "[a]ll these exchanges were conducted in the straightforward conviction that museum professionals operating with complete academic freedom are among the most effective ambassadors between cultures."[15] U.S. museum professionals conducted 245 projects with partners in 85 other countries that were superficially labeled as "successful"; yet when the program was reviewed in 2007, limitations were identified in IPAM's reach and scale. The lack of a wider ripple effect beyond the individuals who were directly working on IPAM projects led AAM and DOS to review and revise their international collaboration. DOS considered how to expand the impact of its cultural and public diplomacy programs in the aftermath of the 9/11 terrorist attacks in 2001, and AAM recognized the need to align this program with the broader trend of museums engaging more deliberately in community engagement. With dual goals of producing more meaningful and sustainable partnerships among museums rather than among individual staff members as well as creating broader community engagement with these projects—and thus expanding their public diplomacy impact—Museums Connect (originally called Museum and Community Collaborations Abroad) was launched in 2008 as the successor to IPAM.

Museums Connect was designed with the objective of engaging wider communities and more people. Individual museums in the United States and abroad were free to originate, create, and apply for Museums Connect grants. If selected through a peer-review system that included museum professionals, past participants, and AAM staff with oversight from DOS's Bureau of Educational and Cultural Affairs (ECA), participating museums were given latitude to operate according to the performance-based outcomes agreed upon during the application and selection phase. Grants were $50,000 to $100,000, with a 50 percent cost share from the participating museums. Because the program's main funder (DOS) is part of the U.S. government and the administrator (AAM) is a U.S.-based organization, each grant was managed by a lead U.S. museum, which was responsible for the grant's financials, compliance, and periodic reporting. This dynamic ensured that the dominant language of the projects' activities and reporting would be American English. Although some changes to the grant program subsequently occurred—including the reduction of project length from two years to one and a name change to Museums Connect in 2011—its principles and aims remained consistent until its final grant cycle concluded in 2017.

As the main funder, DOS ECA intended Museums Connect to operate as one part of a larger public diplomacy agenda grounded in ideas of the nation-state and the promotion of the United States internationally. Unlike shorter-term traditional diplomatic activities between politicians and ambassadors, the goals of U.S. public diplomacy programs such as Museums Connect, Fulbright student and scholar exchanges, DanceMotion USA (which sends U.S. dance groups overseas), and the American Film Showcase (which showcases U.S.-made documentaries around the world) are oriented toward the long-term goal of building good will and affinity toward the United States. DOS states, "The mission of American public diplomacy is to support the achievement of U.S. foreign policy goals and objectives, advance national interests, and enhance national security by informing and influencing foreign publics and by expanding and strengthening the relationship between the people and Government of the United States and citizens of the rest of the world."[16] Museums Connect focused on youth as a strategic audience in countries and regions that DOS deemed to be strategically important for economic and geopolitical reasons and reflected the belief that influencing non-U.S. youth would have a positive long-term effect on the "national interest" of the United States.

Alongside these public diplomacy goals, AAM, which administrated the program, established clear museological goals that made Museums Connect seem distinctly new and ambitious compared to previous domestic programming and IPAM's limited reach. Identifying a lack of wider community engagement as a central limitation of IPAM, AAM reported, "The Museums Connect program strengthens connections and cultural understanding between people in the United States and abroad through innovative projects facilitated by museums and executed by their communities. The program's mission is to build global communities through cross-cultural exchanges while also supporting U.S. foreign policy goals, such as youth empowerment, environmental sustainability and disability rights awareness."[17] These goals emerged not only from the evaluation and reconsideration of the IPAM program but also from changes in how U.S. museums and historic sites engaged with communities and their publics in the twentieth century.

FROM CABINETS OF CURIOSITY TO DIALOGIC MUSEUMS AND INTERNATIONAL PUBLIC HISTORY

Museums Connect represents one example of a much larger and more gradual shift in the theory and practice of U.S. museums.[18] History museums here grew in number during the nineteenth century—"the Century of History."[19] The period was marked by the accumulation of collections and specimens and a growing appreciation for the past, which had the result of dramatically increasing the number of museums around the nation. This idolatry of the past, however, occurred only within elite circles, often in urban society. Museums in the nineteenth century were places where the wealthy wielded interpretive and intellectual authority, which they used as an ideological tool and an instrument of power.[20]

The display and collection of international specimens and peoples were a vehicle of nation-state power. Even the international contexts within World's Fairs traveling exhibitions had the goal of nation making and the reinforcement of societal power hierarchies.[21]

Towards the end of the nineteenth century, American museums began to consider their role as public institutions, and the idea of "the democratic museum" emerged.[22] One of the earliest instances of this shift was recorded in an 1872 *New York Times* article about the Metropolitan Museum of Art, which was attempting to encourage working people to take advantage of a free weekend day at the museum. Although the article's language makes the paternalism of this venture obvious, the goal of the scheme centered around the consumption of the aesthetic and thus its meaning. "Yesterday," the article reported, "the experiment was tried of throwing [the museum] open to the public, without restriction, on Saturdays, and it was expected that there would be a great rush, and that those whose occupations confine them to the desk, or the room, or the counter all the week would joyfully profit by the privilege and attend . . . Unfortunately this result was not arrived at."[23] Similarly, in the 1880s the Smithsonian Institution's assistant secretary in charge of the National Museum, George Brown Goode, embraced the belief that museums could be places to benefit society and serve educational roles. Under Goode's guidance, museum personnel, while maintaining the institution's collection of artifacts, specimens, and art that had once been thought to exude meaning by their presence alone, began to consider what larger knowledge museum objects and artifacts might convey.[24]

The rise of public education was a significant national political issue during the Progressive era at the turn of the twentieth century, and this debate encouraged American museums to use their collections more deliberately and thoughtfully for the education of their audiences.[25] In his 1917 essay "The Gloom of the Museum," John Cotton Dana, founder and director of the Newark Museum, insisted, contrary to conventional thinking, that museums should consider their public function: "Now seems to come the demand that the museum serve its people in the task of helping them to appreciate the high importance of manner, to hold by the laws of simplicity and restraint, and to broaden their sympathies and multiply their interests."[26]

In the early twentieth-century museum, however, this sentiment was only beginning to gain credence. While the impulse to educate was becoming a larger trend, it was not ubiquitous and remained enmeshed in museums' wider ideological and political functions. Many urban historical societies continued to act as gathering places and social clubs for elites long into the twentieth century.[27] As interest in history continued to flourish in the early twentieth-century United States, other types of interpretive sites emerged, including outdoor museums such as Colonial Williamsburg and Greenfield Village as well as units of the National Park Service.[28]

The seeds of change that began in Progressive era art museums faded as American museums began to reflect the economic, political, and societal shifts that took place between the 1930s and 1950s: the economic disarray of the Great Depression, attempts to appeal to traditional art museum visitors who had moved to the newly developed suburbs, and fears of being associated with "the taint of socialism."[29] In response to the civil rights movement and the new social history paradigms of the 1960s, however, as well as to the fracturing of the liberal consensus and the associated culture wars of the 1980s and 1990s, museums—and public historians more broadly—did begin to address the need to democratize the interpretation and exhibition of history and engage others in the history-making enterprise.[30]

These changes were not homogeneously embraced in all U.S. museums. The 1960s and 1970s were also a time when many community and neighborhood African American museums—connected to the politics of the civil rights and black power movements and to larger shifts in African American political and economic power—opened and began to challenge what the African American poet June Jordan lambasted as "ultimately meaningless temples of Euro-American hegemony."[31] These contestations to the dominant, mainstream, national museum culture mirrored similar challenges by Native Americans that manifested in "the Native American Museum movement" and serve as cautions against painting trends in U.S. museums with too broad a brush.[32]

The move to revise traditional museum power relationships gained broader momentum in the final decades of the twentieth century, providing practical and theoretical contexts for the Museums Connect program and the three U.S. museums featured in this book's case studies. In his study of the reconceptualization of power among public historians and museums in the 1980s and 1990s, the oral and public historian Michael Frisch has coined the term *a shared authority*, a phrase that has come to form a central tenet of the practice and study of public history.[33] Grounded in broadly democratic assumptions about the public sphere, Frisch's thesis is a potent descriptor of the way in which historical knowledge became understood in the last quarter of the twentieth century, and it challenged public and oral historians to consider their own position vis-à-vis their power and the public. Yet while his argument is still central to the practice of oral historians, his notion of *a shared authority* has been adapted and employed differently by public historians. Contrary to Frisch's original argument—that authority is inherently shared—the assumption that a public historian *has* authority to share and thus *should be* sharing it with the public has become common in the field and a central part of public history practice. The subtle distinction between Frisch's conception and the prescriptive use that now pervades the public history field reflects different understandings of where the authority in history making lies. Sharing authority may seem to be a benevolent way to include others in the practice of history making, yet it reflects an assumption on the part of public historians that they *possess* the authority to interpret the past: that it is *theirs* to share. As a result, exhibitions, community forums, and community-based programming are often conducted on the terms of the professional public historian, who retains control over the practice of meaning making. Although different public historians apply the concept in different ways and in different contexts, few analyze or interrogate the idea of sharing authority as a paternalistic practice.

Frisch has recognized the misuse of his original conception and has since revisited the idea.[34] Nonetheless, as a mode of public history, sharing authority has been widely embraced and has shaped the field as well as the scholarship and practices that informed the 2008 creation of Museums Connect. In the decades since Frisch published his original study, many museums and historic sites have incorporated his ideas and have attempted to move toward the idea of the forum—a seminal notion that Duncan Cameron introduced twenty years before Frisch's theory of shared authority—and beyond institutional legacies in which museums act as the sole author of the past. In so doing they engage their publics in many different ways—for instance, by considering their interpretations and perspectives of the past and allowing dialogue and dispute to occur within an institution's once-hallowed walls.[35] One important outcome of this larger rethinking of the intellectual underpinnings of museums has been a shift in the way in which museums think about and engage with their local communities and the role that they play in fostering an inclusive civil society.[36] The focus on communities has also influenced the highest levels of the profession in the United States, resulting, for instance, in the AAM's 1998 Museums and Community Initiative, a signal of the importance that communities had gained in the language of museums. This was accompanied by a range of new guidelines and scholarship that considered the opportunities, challenges, and implications of reorienting public history and museum practices toward communities.

One tangible outgrowth of this shift has been a growing acceptance of the concept of the *dialogic museum*. The idea of a public historian as a facilitator rather than a knowledge giver decenters institutional authority, placing dialogue at the center of public history and requiring public historians to bring a different set of skills to their practice.[37] The Lower East Side Tenement Museum in New York City, for example, has transformed its practice and relationship to expertise and knowledge and has introduced dialogic programming to connect visitors to the history of immigration that the site interprets. Small facilitator-led dialogic programs encourage visitors to challenge their preconceived stereotypes and consider the contemporary ramifications of New York's immigrant history.[38] Around the United States, a number of other historic sites have also attempted to rethink the relationship between place and the immigrant communities that those places represent.[39] According to the scholars Katharine Corbett and Dick Miller, "shared inquiry" should be at the center of reflective public history practice. That is, all participants should be able to share questions, guide the direction of inquiry, and truly practice a communal exploration of the past, even if they desire different outcomes from the process.[40] These theoretical changes have directly affected public history practice and are changing power relationships between public historians and the public. Yet even though the trend is now dominant in the United States, the evolution of practice and the way in which museums and public historians view history making vis-à-vis the public should not be misunderstood as a homogeneous shift among *all* U.S. museums. Rather, this evolution is occurring sporadically as museums respond to their local political, social, and economic landscapes.

TOWARD A NEW SET OF TRANSNATIONAL PUBLIC HISTORY PRACTICES

In recent years a developing body of scholarship around public history in postcolonial contexts has merged these new modi operandi for public historians with the recent internationalization of the field.[41] These studies have energized the nascent field of scholarship that seeks to analyze, categorize, and take stock of the international turn.[42] This book joins that field in its focus on Museums Connect. Growing out of the American museological and public history contexts, the program stood, during its existence, at the intersection of the current international turn in public history and the movement of public history sites, institutions, and practitioners toward engaging more inclusively and democratically with community partners. Museums Connect partnered U.S. and non-U.S. museums and their communities and demonstrated unique community engagement dynamics both locally and transnationally that starkly highlighted embedded power differentials. In this way, it revealed the challenges and potential of strategies developed and implemented to mitigate entrenched hierarchies of power in community-focused public history programming.

Increasingly, museums, historic sites, university faculty, classes, and public history institutions are searching for projects and programming that attempt to co-create the past with historically marginalized individuals, groups, and communities and to overcome historical-institutional silences. I argue that history making—through exhibitions and programming—can minimize and mitigate international hierarchies and barriers of power through deliberately reflective practice that interrogates individual and institutional authority—codified in sharing authority—from the outset. Care is required, however, to ensure that this important but hard-to-navigate work is handled delicately and that historical hierarchies of power are not reinforced.

Given the heterogeneity of the museum field and the diverse range of institutional, local, and individual contexts informing Museums Connect projects, these strategies neither claim to be definitive nor to be the only ways to negotiate transnational public history power hierarchies. Rather, they represent a range of strategies that institutions, their staff, and their community partners deliberately—and sometimes accidentally—employed to successfully respond to different local contexts and situations within their projects to mitigate hierarchies of power baked into Museums Connect and created by the actions and decisions of the participating institutions and their staff, especially the assumption of authority by U.S. museum professionals and public historians.

In studying the opportunities and potential pitfalls of strategies used to navigate these power differentials, our understanding of how best to challenge, negotiate, and mitigate museums' and public historians' institutional authority is advanced. Shining a light on museum-community collaborations within a wider transnational frame demonstrates effective strategies to overcome power hierarchies in local and domestic contexts where political, social, and economic differentials may be less immediately obvious. At the core of Museums Connect and institutional public history work more broadly, however, is the negotiation of institutional behaviors and actions by marginalized communities. Understanding and embracing the exciting possibility that comes from this recognition—and allowing for negotiation in institutional practices—open our practice to become more relevant to communities, to gain greater community buy-in, and to continue to de-center the authority and power of public history practitioners and institutions in community history making. In so doing, our institutions, knowing that the barriers to a truly democratic institution-community relationship exist and will never be truly eradicated but continuously challenged and pushed against from within and without, can move further down the road toward becoming inclusive, democratic, and more relevant to historically marginalized communities.

This book focuses on three Museums Connect partnerships between museums in the United States and museums in Afghanistan, Morocco, and South Africa, using them as case studies for analyzing the practical and theoretical implications of transnational public history. An examination of their diverse geographical and geopolitical contexts as well as their different public history practices allows us to understand the multifaceted social, political, and economic imperatives that shaped and directed Museums Connect projects and to assess their successes and shortcomings. Chapter 1 elucidates the specific conditions in the fields of public history and public diplomacy that gave rise to the program. Chapter 2 looks at the way in which local political contexts and public history and memory-making practices shaped Museums Connect collaborations between the National Constitution Center in Philadelphia and the National Museum of Afghanistan in Kabul. Chapter 3 focuses on the use of transnational public history pedagogy in the projects shared between the Museum of History and Holocaust Education at Kennesaw State University in Georgia and the Ben M'sik Community Museum at University Hassan II in Casablanca. Chapter 4 considers the International Youth Legacy Leadership project conducted between the Birmingham Civil Rights Institute in Alabama and the Nelson Mandela House Museum and the Apartheid Museum in Johannesburg. The book concludes with a discussion about how these programs shed light on Museums Connect as a new type of transnational public history that can help us understand the essential democratic and inclusive underpinnings of museum-community partnerships.

CHAPTER 1

"State Department Museums"?

The Convergence and Divergence of Public Diplomacy and Public History

After the announcement of the Museums and Communities Collaboration Abroad (MCCA) program in July 2007, Steven Inskeep, the host of National Public Radio's *Morning Edition*, interviewed Erik Ledbetter, AAM's director of international programs, and Lee Rosenbaum, a cultural critic, about the overt and (in Rosenbaum's eyes) insidious use of U.S. museums as vehicles for public diplomacy. Inskeep provocatively opened the segment by suggesting that "[s]ome people who run American museums are asking if they want to be used to promote foreign policy" before cutting to excerpts from separate interviews he had already conducted with his two sources.[1] In her response, Rosenbaum focused on the fact that DOS had offered suggestions for geographical and thematic areas to be considered in the first round of grants. "Certainly," she said, "there has been a history of government support for exhibitions going abroad. But the proposals generally and the planning and the concepts behind the exhibition should come from the museums and not be dictated by the federal government." Ledbetter clarified that it would be "colleagues, U.S. scholars, not administration officials who will make the final awards."[2] But Rosenbaum's critique of MCCA (which would later become Museums Connect) had only begun. In a blog post reflecting on the radio segment, she asked, "Does this mean that institutions that imprudently allow themselves [to] be co-opted by political propagandists will henceforth be known as 'State Department Museums'?"[3]

As Rosenbaum's comments reveal, the idea that U.S. museums might operate as vehicles for government-sponsored cultural diplomatic programs can be polarizing. Many people fear the encroachment of the government into every sphere of their lives and consider governmental foreign policy, however it is enacted, to be insidious and imperialistic. Rosenbaum's critique of MCCA's launch was relatively localized, based on the misperception that DOS was dictating which museums would receive funding. But it was also predicated on the false assumption that U.S. museums are apolitical and divorced from ideological and power considerations—a view that does not fit into the long history of American and European museums.

The birth of the modern western museum in the nineteenth century was intimately connected to the solidification of the nation-state's power over the public. Since then, museums have grappled with their roles vis-à-vis the people.[4] The idea of the democratic museum and the civic role of museums that emerged at the end of that century had a long and complex genealogy. Likewise, public history sites and museums in the latter half of the twentieth century evolved gradually—and certainly not homogeneously—away from the projection and demonstration of authority, the belief that the public is monolithic and passively receives culture and education, the definition of the self against a foreign other, and toward the democratization of the interpretation and exhibition of the past.[5] Only by the last decades of the century did this notion gain momentum.[6]

This public history evolution was not the only context within which Museums Connect was created. As a DOS program, it also had a public diplomacy agenda. Public diplomacy had been evolving since World War II, and the department's use of museums and exhibitions in foreign policy was an important practice during the Cold War. In other words, there were parallels between public diplomacy's idea of people-to-people connections and public history's move toward the forum, community engagement, and dialogism. Both public diplomacy and community-engaged public history saw value in placing individuals and communities in conversation.

Museums Connect was created in 2007 because DOS ECA and AAM had similar short-term motivations to expand the impact of IPAM and reach more individuals and communities. As with many grant programs, however, the agenda of the major sponsor—in this instance, DOS ECA—became central. Even though its conception, approach to awarding grants, and control of grants during their operation were based on exchange, dialogue, and collaborative relationships, Museum Connect's central goal was to improve U.S. standing in the world. This goal jarred with the public history paradigm that formed AAM's rationale for the program's creation and provided its model of project operation: that the power and authority of meaning making are not the sole purview of the institution.[7] Of course, it is never possible to entirely flatten power differentials, but AAM's impulse to engage the public in collaborative history making nonetheless grated against DOS's people-to-people diplomacy goals.

SOFT POWER, PUBLIC DIPLOMACY, AND THE POWER OF PEOPLE-TO-PEOPLE DIPLOMACY

Even in their early years, American museums were explicitly political, but that political role increased significantly immediately after World War II, when they became a Cold War vehicle for foreign policy. During the first half of the 1940s, the U.S. government was already beginning to explore new ways to further its interests abroad by engaging foreign nations and people through a broad range of public diplomacy pursuits, but it did not formally adopt this approach until 1948. At that point public diplomacy became an important method for pushing the nation's soft power agenda alongside the more traditional efforts of politicians, ambassadors, and diplomats. The term *soft power,* while useful in this discussion, is an anachronism; Joseph Nye, a former assistant secretary of defense in the Clinton administration, did not coin the term until 1990. He defined it as "the ability to get what you want through attraction rather than coercion or payments. It arises from the attractiveness of a country's culture, political ideals, and policies. When our policies are seen as legitimate in the eyes of others, our soft power is enhanced . . . When you can get others to admire your ideals and to want what you want, you do not have to spend as much on sticks and carrots to move them in your direction." After the 9/11 terrorist attacks, he noted that ideas of soft power are motivated by the ideas of "attraction and seduction." Nye suggested that U.S. officials had erred too far in the direction of hard power—that to be most effective, soft power must work hand in hand with hard power (the carrots and sticks) to advance America's interests in global affairs. Given the United States' significant and assertive involvement in global affairs since the end of World War II, his argument has considerable salience.[8]

Still, stakeholders did not always agree on how to define and implement public diplomacy. According to Nye, a division emerged between "those who favored the slow media of cultural diplomacy—art, books, exchanges—that had a trickle-down effect, and those who favored the fast information media of radio, movies, and newsreels, which promised more immediate and visible 'bang for the buck.'" These debates reflected public diplomacy throughout the twentieth century, "proponents of these two approaches struggled over how the government should invest in soft power. The 'tough-minded' did not shy away from direct propaganda while the 'tender-minded' argued that changing international attitudes is a gradual process that needs to be measured in years" and occurs through meetings with individual citizens and conversational engagement with wider publics. There were also disagreements over how free of government control government-supported programs should be. Nye argued that, despite the success of Cold War–era policies and programs, which made America attractive to citizens in Eastern Europe, the Soviet Union, and China, this debate remains unresolved because both sides of the argument are valid.[9]

During the Cold War, the United States effectively implemented soft power through public diplomacy. The seeds for this work were laid in the early 1940s when, as the nation entered World War II, the U.S. Information Service (USIS) and other government agencies used radio—particularly the Voice of America—art exhibitions, and libraries in Europe and Central and South America to positively influence international public opinion.[10] In the subsequent transition into the Cold War, the importance of spreading the U.S. message to non-U.S. publics gained greater urgency as the nation took the lead in rebuilding war-ravaged Europe and countering negative Soviet propaganda about the inadequacies of the United States and, by extension, capitalism.

In practice, the implementation of cultural diplomacy was messy and contradictory. Agencies employed a range of cultural forms in a variety of contexts, including architecture, reading rooms, book translations, publications, libraries, and scholar and student exchanges, in order to project U.S. interests abroad, counter anti-U.S. propaganda, and shine a glow on the nation's politics and culture. The U.S. Information Agency (USIA), the successor to the U.S. Information Service, was specifically created to centralize these disparate cultural and public diplomacy activities and present U.S. cultural products as a vehicle for effectively attracting support for the country's "culture, political ideals and policies."[11]

USIS libraries and librarians were exported as early as 1942 to spread English-language publications, provide alternatives to closed societies and nations that restricted access to certain works, and disseminate pro-U.S. propaganda. In 1943 the U.S. embassy in London opened two reading rooms, and by 1955 USIS-ALA (American Library Association) libraries were common in most major cities of the world. Books translated into English were exported to these government libraries, and by 1963 250,000 books were leaving the United States each year.[12]

The Central Intelligence Agency (CIA) operated a program in Western Europe in the early years of the Cold War that attempted to influence and ensure that the intelligentsia in those countries supported the growth of U.S. interests in the region and were not tempted by Eastern Europe's flourishing communism.[13] Beyond such deliberately planned cultural diplomacy activities, other cultural forms also came to symbolize the United States internationally. The rapid increase in construction of U.S. embassies across the globe exported a new U.S. architectural style that stood in stark contrast to Soviet architectural forms, and the historian and cultural diplomat Richard Arndt argues that this played a significant role in establishing a globally interventionist United States across the globe: "The symbolism of the American buildings was anything but imperial—yet they connoted a new kind of empire."[14]

Such expressions of *pax Americana* were not without contradictions and ambivalence. The Cold War jazz tours between 1956 and 1974 revealed some of the challenges that the government faced in attempting to use citizens, especially African American musicians in the era before civil rights legislation, to project U.S. values abroad. The government confidently believed that such tours would lead audiences to wish to change their own countries in order to reflect the supposedly multicultural image of the United States. Yet the tours were built on an unresolved paradox and were challenged by African American musicians who did not live in this artificial color-blind paradise, which limited their effectiveness and invited challenges to the U.S. image.[15]

Such "tough-minded" approaches to public diplomacy co-existed with more exchange-based, "person-to-person contacts." Public Law 402, the United States Information and Educational Exchange Act, was one of the first manifestations of a "tender-minded" approach to soft power.[16] Also known as the Smith-Mundt Act, the law was passed on January 27, 1948, "to promote the better understanding of the United States among the peoples of the world and to strengthen cooperative international relations."[17] The objective was "to enable the Government of the United States to promote a better understanding of the United States in other countries, and to increase mutual understanding between the people of the United States and the people of other countries."[18] When President Harry S. Truman approved the act, he committed the government to conducting information, education, and cultural exchange activities on a worldwide, long-term scale during a time of peace.[19]

The 1961 Mutual Educational and Cultural Exchange Act, commonly called the Fulbright-Hays Act, extended these goals even further. The apogee of the idea of exchange and people-to-people diplomacy, the act continues to be seen as a justification for educational and cultural exchanges. It was intended to "enable the Government of the United States to increase mutual understanding between the people of the United States and the people of other countries by means of educational and cultural exchange." The act's sponsors hoped such exchanges would

> strengthen the ties which unite us with other nations by demonstrating the educational and cultural interests, developments, and achievements of the people of the United States and other nations, and the contributions being made toward a peaceful and more fruitful life for people throughout the world; to promote international cooperation for educational and cultural advancement; and thus to assist in the development of friendly, sympathetic, and peaceful relations between the United States and the other countries of the world.[20]

In other words, by connecting U.S. and non-U.S. citizens through cultural and educational programs, the United States hoped to tacitly recruit the support of international audiences for its many foreign policy agendas. Or, as one commentator suggested, the act would at least give the United States the benefit of the doubt.[21]

A belief in the power of citizen exchanges as expressed in the Smith-Mundt and Fulbright-Hays acts formed a central justification for those who preferred a "tender-minded" approach to public diplomacy rather than a more overtly propagandistic one. Yet neither mode operated within a vacuum. As Arndt points out, "[i]n projecting their cultures, groups and nation states from the beginning of history had insisted on balance, on 'exchanges,' on reciprocity, and on bidirectional flow."[22] Still, those who frame public diplomacy as a way to use the inherent values and virtues of U.S. culture to counter negative opinions of the nation have consistently drawn on those important pieces of legislation. A 1985 report by the U.S. Advisory Commission on Public Diplomacy suggested that "[p]ublic diplomacy supplements and reinforces traditional diplomacy by explaining U.S. policies to foreign publics, by providing them with information about American society and culture."[23] In 1989 the National War College fellow Paul A. Smith reflected on the intimate connection between cultural and public diplomacy and other types of foreign policy and international relations: "[Public diplomacy] seeks to elicit popular support for solutions of mutual benefit that avoids [*sic*] threats, compulsion, or intimidation. It is not a form of political warfare, although it may be used in combination with political warfare."[24] DOS's 2004 "Report of the Advisory Committee on Cultural Diplomacy" clarified the rationale behind the use of culture within public diplomacy: "Cultural diplomacy is the linchpin of public diplomacy; for it is in cultural activities that a nation's idea of itself is best represented."

> Cultural diplomacy is a two-way street: for every foreign artist inspired by an American work of art, there is an American waiting to be touched by the creative wonders of other traditions. Culture spreads from individual to individual, often by subterranean means; in exchange programs like Fulbright, Humphrey, and Muskie, in person-to-person contacts made

> possible by international visitor and student exchange programs, ideas that we hold dear—of family, education, and faith—cross borders, creating new ways of thinking.[25]

The report concluded: "Indeed the ideals of the Founding Fathers, enshrined in the Declaration of Independence, the Constitution, the Federalist Papers, and the Bill of Rights, take on new life in the vibrant traditions of American art, dance, film, jazz and literature, which continue to inspire people the world over despite our political differences."[26] In other words, as Nancy Snow summarized, "to know us, is to like us."[27]

John Lenczowski, a senior DOS public diplomacy official in 2007, supported the use of culture as one method of public diplomacy. Reflecting on the notion that exchange and people-to-people diplomacy must operate in connection with other types of public diplomacy, he argued that "cultural diplomacy can be integrated with other elements of these activities whether they be in the realm of information policy, ideological competition, countering hostile propaganda, foreign aid policy, religious democracy, or establishing relationships of trust." Thus, "in these capacities, cultural diplomacy can have positive effects on foreign cooperation with U.S. policy."[28] Entrenched within such views is the belief that public diplomacy, in whichever mode it is practiced, can positively affect U.S. global standing, create affinity for the nation among global populations, and act in conjunction with traditional diplomacy and hard power to reinforce American global hegemony. Indeed, in her confirmation address before the Senate Foreign Relations Committee in 2013, Evan Ryan, then the assistant secretary of state for educational and cultural affairs, explained, "When you meet Americans, you meet American values."[29] Implicit yet broadly understood within this statement is the belief that "meet[ing] American values" will naturally persuade and convince skeptical audiences to understand, forgive, give the benefit of the doubt to, or collaborate with the apparently homogeneous United States on any number of complex foreign policy objectives or projects.

MUSEUMS AND SOFT POWER

The use of museums as a tool for international affairs and the projection of national power began with the international exhibitions and worlds' fairs of the late nineteenth and early twentieth centuries.[30] The idea gained momentum in the 1940s, just as the United States was adopting a more active role in international geopolitics and its government was beginning to explore the virtues of public diplomacy and soft power. In 1942, within the fraught international context of World War II, Theodore Low, an educator at the Metropolitan Museum of Art, urged museums to become central educational institutions. In an essay commissioned by AAM, he argued that "the museum as an already established institution with vast resources of material of all kinds and description must take its place beside the library as a bulwark of the movement for popular education."[31] Significantly, Low identified the important role that U.S. museums could play in foreign policy:

> No one can deny that museums have powers which are of the utmost importance in any war of ideologies. They have the power to make people see the truth, the power to make people recognize the importance of the individual as a member of society, and, of equal importance in combating subversive inroads, the power to keep minds happy and healthy. They have, in short, propaganda powers which should be more effective in their truth and eternal character than those of the Axis which are based on falsehoods and half-truths. Museums with the potentiality of reaching millions of our citizens must not fail to recognize their responsibility.[32]

Even though the United States soon began using other cultural forms as part of its soft-power approach to international diplomacy, the government was haphazard about employing exhibitions and object exchanges until IPAM was created in 1980. Nonetheless, the empty walls of USIA libraries, embassies, and cultural affairs offices did serve as venues for a range of art exhibitions, of varying size and quality, that were intended to demonstrate the virtues of U.S. culture while, by removing language barriers, providing international audiences with an easy method of engagement. As Arndt notes, the export of U.S. art in the decades after World War II was "clumsy." Congress often resisted it, citing concerns about cost and the image that U.S. modern art might spread abroad. Still, during the 1950s and 1960s a steady flow of art left the United States to travel the world, thanks to USIA art director David Scott, himself a museum professional. This activity culminated in 1965 with the creation of the International Arts Program (IAP), a partnership between USIA and the Smithsonian Institution.[33] IAP experimented with buying prints of work and sending out multiple versions of inexpensive exhibitions to embassies and libraries across the globe.

Exporting art exhibitions was not solely the purview of the U.S. government. For instance, the Museum of Modern Art used traveling exhibitions to expand its influence beyond New York City, most notably with *The Family of Man*, an influential 1955 photography exhibit that the museum called "a forthright declaration of global solidarity in the decade following World War II." Its catalogue was translated into dozens of languages, and the exhibition was reproduced fifteen times by USIA. It traveled extensively in other countries, including West Germany (at the urging of the diplomat Paul Cushing Child) and the Soviet Union.[34] Although no other exhibition matched *The Family of Man* in its reception—3 million copies of the catalogue were sold—a 1963 contemporary art exhibition of one hundred paintings curated by Dore Ashton traveled to East Asia with the support of USIA, where it received significant acclaim.[35] Yet as the historian Michael Krenn highlights how art as a form of cultural diplomacy met stiff criticism at home, where definitions of what was and was not American art elicited strong opinions and stormy debates, and political oversight ultimately limited the effectiveness of traveling exhibitions.[36]

Object-based exhibitions were also used to communicate U.S. values and interests abroad. For instance, the 1956 *Atoms for Peace* exhibit presented the atomic age in a positive light and was warmly received by 100,000 visitors in Hiroshima. In 1959 the American National Exhibition, part of a 1958 U.S.-U.S.S.R. cultural exchange agreement, traveled to the Soviet Union with the propagandistic goal of persuading Soviet citizens that the United States had virtues.[37] Other countries also used traveling exhibitions as a mode of "tough-minded" public diplomacy. This tendency increased in the 1970s and 1980s, when a number of nations put together national-treasures exhibitions as a way to influence the thinking and actions of global audiences. However, the foreign policy impact was marginal at best.[38]

Traveling exhibitions as vehicles for international boosterism continued after the end of the Cold War. *Mexico: Splendors of Thirty Centuries* traveled in the United States in 1990–91, and Turkey and Indonesia had significant traveling exhibitions in the late 1980s and early 1990s. Following the 9/11 terrorist attacks, the United States sent a photographic exhibit of Ground Zero around the globe in an attempt to maintain its hold on international sympathy.[39] This use of traveling exhibitions to purvey a manufactured positive view of a nation mimics the efforts of many domestic museums to promote positive images of their communities' histories.[40]

In addition to such actively propagandistic uses, U.S. museums also became vehicles for "tender-minded" approaches of exchange, evolving, in the late 1970s and early 1980s, toward engaging their communities rather than acting only as purveyors.[41] A seeming confluence between people-to-people diplomacy and the new ideology of the museum as an outward-facing forum emerged as ideas about the function and role of museums in U.S. society began to change. The apparent similarities between these two practices gave birth to IPAM in 1980. Administered by AAM and funded by DOS, the program, unlike traveling exhibitions that ignored dialogue in favor of projecting values and ideas, sponsored "one-to-one projects, connecting one curator, or one researcher, in a location with their counterpart."[42] These year-long people-to-people exchanges allowed a museum staff member to travel to a colleague's country to collaborate on a variety of different projects. Heather Berry, the former manager of international programs at AAM, recalled, "There were dinosaur digs, there were people looking at telescopes, and we had a great partnership with a gentleman at the Adler Planetarium in Chicago working with a museum in Germany and they went through old collections and were able to find these old telescopes that people had not even realized . . . were in their collections. They'd been sitting in the corner in this wooden box with some lenses, and they were able to find these."[43] Over the course of twenty-seven years, IPAM sponsored 245 partnerships connecting U.S. museum professionals with eighty-five countries around the world.[44] Yet it was limited in its impact. Although the projects produced exhibitions and scholarship, they were retroactively criticized for more frequently benefiting individual curators and scholars' intellectual and academic interests than the participants' institutions or broader communities.[45] Because each grant was limited to two museum professionals, IPAM's diplomacy agenda was also limited in its impact. The costs were relatively low, and the projects received little attention during an otherwise tumultuous period of upheaval and change within the U.S. approach to public diplomacy.

"GENERALLY APATHETIC"

In the early 1990s the culture wars and a public dispute over the perceived politicization of historical narratives and history making were raging in the United States. At the same time public historians were rethinking power and authority as the Cold War came to an end and the nation emerged from a half-century-long ideological conflict.[46] The victorious atmosphere in the United States was creating a complacency among politicians, giving them a rationale for limiting government spending, which had risen significantly since the 1940s. Without any apparent need for public diplomacy, in either "tough-minded" or "tender-minded" forms, Congress voted for heavy spending cuts in USIA and other government programs. Mary Jeffers, a long-time USIA and DOS public affairs officer and later a public diplomacy fellow at George Washington University, emphasized the lack of importance placed on public diplomacy programs at the end of the Cold War: "USIA experienced severe budget cuts . . . [W]e used to do a lot of things that are not that different from what we're doing today, and then we went into a period of doing very little of them because we had very little money."[47] To understand the significant decline in emphasis on public diplomacy and the fear that all those involved felt at the end of the Cold War, one need only read the Government Accountability Office report of September 23, 1996:

> To sustain a major reduction, USIA may have to consider closing more posts than it presently plans in countries where USIA has determined that the United States has limited public diplomacy goals. The impact of such closures now and in the future is uncertain. Another option would be to reconfigure USIA's overseas presence, which is currently based on a structure established after World War II. For example, USIA maintains

> cultural centers and branch offices (that provide basic information on the United States and counsel students interested in attending U.S. schools) in countries that previously did not, but now have access to other sources of information on the United States. These options have the potential to substantially reduce costs.[48]

As this excerpt suggests, USIA officials were pleading with those in charge of government appropriations to acknowledge the need for a robust and well-funded public diplomacy program. The entire document exudes the sense that further reductions in USIA's budget would have been deadly to the U.S. foreign policy agenda. Arthur A. Bados, a retired USIA foreign service officer, echoed the report's bleak tone in a 2001 essay. Writing about USIA's merger with DOS in 1999, he lamented, "If public diplomacy has to give up its hard-won culture and is made to adopt that of the Department of State, it will languish until someday a new political accident again lodges it in a separate entity. Americans of good will who spent most of their lives learning and creating this new profession must hope that it will not come to that."[49] Thus, even though there was strong political determination to balance the budget while celebrating the U.S. "victory" in the Cold War, these two inside accounts remind us that many felt that public diplomacy was just as important after the fall of the Berlin Wall (1989–90) as it had been before.

Anyone listening to Bill Clinton's first inaugural address in 1993, whether they were ordinary citizens, diplomats, or USIA officials, may have believed that the public diplomacy agenda was about to become a more important aspect of U.S. foreign affairs:

> To renew America, we must meet challenges abroad as well as at home. There is no longer a clear division between what is foreign and what is domestic. The world economy, the world environment, the world AIDS crisis, the world arms race: they affect us all. Today, as an older order passes, the new world is more free but less stable. Communism's collapse has called forth old animosities and new dangers. Clearly, America must continue to lead the world we did so much to make.
>
> While America rebuilds at home, we will not shrink from the challenges nor fail to seize the opportunities of this new world. Together with our friends and allies, we will work to shape change, lest it engulf us. When our vital interests are challenged or the will and conscience of the

> international community is defied, we will act, with peaceful diplomacy whenever possible, with force when necessary. The brave Americans serving our Nation today in the Persian Gulf, in Somalia, and wherever else they stand are testament to our resolve. But our greatest strength is the power of our ideas, which are still new in many lands. Across the world we see them embraced, and we rejoice. Our hopes, our hearts, our hands are with those on every continent who are building democracy and freedom. Their cause is America's cause.[50]

Clinton's touting of "peaceful diplomacy whenever possible" as well as his exaltation of the "power of ideas" suggested a move away from hard power toward softer means. Yet in reality, the Clinton administration's larger view of public diplomacy was, in the words of the historian and political commentator Walter Laqueur, "generally apathetic."[51] As spending on public diplomacy was cut to help balance the federal budget, cultural diplomacy programs dramatically shrank in number and scale, despite protests and warnings from bureaucrats and USIA attachés. USIA's budget peaked at $1.084 billion in 1992 before declining to $450 million in 1997; it grew again slightly to $475 million in 1999.[52] Amid this focus on streamlining and reducing inefficiencies, USIA and its public diplomacy programs were merged into DOS in 1999.[53]

Accounts of public diplomacy efforts after the end of the Cold War are riddled with laments about missed opportunities and ill-informed celebrations of U.S. vitality and its success in spreading democracy around the world. Writing in 1994, Laqueur predicted that it would take certain events to jolt government action back toward public diplomacy:

> There is always the possibility that a major international crisis will have a salutary effect, doing away with delusions about the state of the world, generating greater awareness of the dangers facing America, and putting an end to lethargy and indifference. But such a crisis might be years off, and in the meantime some words of warning are appropriate. The international agenda tends to ignore the concerns of Washington legislators, just as they tend to ignore events outside their bailiwicks. Various clocks are ticking away, irrespective of whether people want to listen to them.[54]

Laqueur's prediction was apt. While IPAM remained relatively unscathed during these larger seismic shifts in public diplomacy, it took a major international crisis to energize conversations about national spending on public diplomacy. These debates, as well as a new focus on how programs would be measured and evaluated, formed the immediate context for the creation of Museums Connect.

"WHY DO THEY HATE US?"

The 9/11 terrorist attacks forced the United States to reconsider the nature of its public diplomacy agenda. During a statement to a joint session of Congress on September 20, 2001, just nine days after the attacks, President George W. Bush asked, "Why do they hate us?"[55] His inquiry reflected a new but very real concern about the opinions of non-U.S. citizens who, by way of the Internet and social media, were gaining a voice in global affairs. Bush, however, answered his own question: "They hate what they see right here in this chamber: a democratically elected government. Their leaders are self-appointed. They hate our freedoms: our freedom of religion, our freedom of speech, our freedom to vote and assemble and disagree with each other."[56] His words suggested that his administration was less interested in exploring real answers to the question than in prescribing its own rationale and continuing the project of exporting U.S. ideas of democracy.

An ensuing public debate brought issues of public diplomacy, as well as its constituent parts (for instance, cultural diplomacy), into the national spotlight and drove a wider governmental review of foreign policy priorities. This debate continued as U.S. involvement in the so-called War on Terror escalated in subsequent years.[57] A 2005 DOS report argued that "the invasion of Iraq, the prisoner abuse scandal at Abu Ghraib, and the controversy over the handling of detainees at Bagram and Guantanamo Bay . . . diminishes [*sic*] our ability to champion freedom, democracy, and individual dignity" and that "culture matters." It continued: "Now that we are at war again, interest in cultural diplomacy is on the rise."[58] Writing during these years, Arndt noted that cultural diplomacy "costs amazingly little, a shadow of the cost of one wing of fighter aircraft."[59] Yet he lamented, "Decently applied over the last six decades, in continuity with the past, and at some reasonable level of quantity, a decent cultural diplomacy might have made a difference, at little cost. It is surely the only element of foreign diplomatic activity which over that time frame might have slowed and perhaps softened the relentless U.S. slide to pariah-dom."[60]

The commitment of DOS, as seen through shifts in funding for ECA since 2001, only partially reflected the urgent public need for a reevaluation of cultural diplomacy. The rapid growth of funding for ECA, from $204 million in 2001 to a peak of $635 million in 2010 (it subsequently decreased to $576 million in 2014), occurred at the same time that the entire DOS budget rose from $27.2 billion to $42.3 billion. (The department's budget reached a peak of $52.6 billion in 2009 before being reduced significantly in 2012.)[61] Thus, ECA's funding fluctuated between 0.7 percent and 1.5 percent of the total DOS budget between 2002 and 2012, with no pattern linked to the rises and falls in the percentage of the total budget. Indeed, while more dollars were being spent on exchange programs, the government's spending on foreign affairs escalated significantly as the United States exited a post–Cold War era of relative global peace and financial restraint and entered one that featured aggressive U.S. global engagement and foreign policy spending, including on other public diplomacy programs that embraced more overtly propagandistic approaches. The George W. Bush administration's first DOS budget request, written in 2001, reflected these changing dynamics:

> This is a time of great opportunity for America—a time, as President Bush has said, to shape "a balance of power that favors freedom." To do this will require good leadership. We have the requisite power and the tools at hand, from our exceptional corps of diplomats to our sturdy battalions of men and women in uniform, from our superb business people to our brilliant artists in every field . . . In past years, the State Department's share of the Federal budget has not been what it should be. With a new Secretary on board, that is changing.[62]

Although the impact of greater investment in public diplomacy allowed for a surge in spending on all types of public and cultural diplomacy programs, the public rhetoric emphasizing efficiency in spending also continued.

Political scientist James McCormick argues that, after 9/11, Congress fell into line behind the White House on matters of foreign policy, offering obedient support for aggressive military options. Nonetheless, members of Congress did publicly urge new and more efficient approaches to the practice of public diplomacy.[63] In July 2005 Senator Richard G. Lugar, a Republican from Indiana and chair of the Senate Foreign Relations Committee, offered the following assessment of public diplomacy in his opening statement at the nomination hearing for Karen Hughes as under secretary of state for public diplomacy: "In an era when allied cooperation is essential in the war against terrorism, negative public opinion overseas has enormous consequences. The Ranking Member and I have observed for some time the unfortunate irony of American public diplomacy efforts. We have asked how the United States can be 'all thumbs' at diplomacy when we are so expert at the strategy and tactics of public relations, marketing and advertising."[64] He went on to chastise the state of public diplomacy as "dysfunctional and requir[ing] major reform." He concluded by offering his support for Hughes:

> This Committee stands ready to ensure that the position of Undersecretary of State for Public Diplomacy has the power, the funding, and the political support required to do the job. We have backed increased funds for public diplomacy, but these funds will have to be spent efficiently if we are to explain clearly the views of the United States, successfully display the humanity and generosity of our citizens, and expand opportunities for interaction between Americans and foreign peoples. Creative thinking will be required.[65]

Lugar's statement, while possibly the public pronouncement expected of Washington politicians, suggested a desire to reengage the world with the supposedly productive, efficient, and effective public diplomacy of both types, as outlined by Nye. The ultimate goal was clearly to project values and ideas abroad and to correct the "all thumbs" approach previously exhibited by DOS. Within this political and economic context, the final cycle of the first IPAM program occurred (2005–7), and the decision to transition to Museum and Community Collaborations Abroad (MCCA) was conceptualized and created.

MUSEUMS AND COMMUNITY COLLABORATIONS ABROAD

Political bluster and television punditry may have driven public discussion about the role of cultural and public diplomacies in post-9/11 U.S. foreign policy, but economic and practical concerns at DOS drove the initial decision to revamp the IPAM program. While the decision to change the program was rigorously vetted by the department and signed off at the assistant secretary level, the true impetus came from Karen Lea Perez, the director of citizen exchanges (2003–8) and a longtime USIA and DOS officer. As she explained, "[w]e were not getting enough diplomatically from a much smaller investment in IPAM."[66] This was undoubtedly a consideration, given the larger discourse about efficiency that permeated all government decision-making during the decade. While serving as the cultural counselor at the U.S. embassy in Paris in 1999–2003, Perez had become familiar with the French Regional and American Museum Exchange (FRAME) program, which changed her thinking about museums as sites for public diplomacy. According to FRAME's website, the program "fosters partnerships among its member museums to develop innovative exhibitions, educational and public programs, and professional exchanges among museum staff, and maintains a bilingual website to reach global audiences."[67] Perez recalled her evolving thought process after observing the FRAME program: "As museum directors met and discussed how they might work together, the completely different structure of decision-making and governance in the two museum communities resulted in several misunderstandings. Those were, of course, sorted out among this group of directors, but I became much more conscious of the prime role of the 'community' in making cultural decisions in the U.S."[68]

At the twenty-year reunion of the Robert Morris Hunt cultural exchange program, at which French and U.S. participants conversed about the relative merits and shortcomings of the two countries' approaches to heritage preservation, Perez solidified her "thinking about new directions that we [DOS] might take in sponsoring museum partnerships." She recalled, "It seemed to me that the nature of American community participation in museums in our country fit well into a broader pattern of volunteerism and civil society that could represent, and reflect, the diversity of our society as a whole."[69] Before returning to Washington, DC, to assume her new role as the director of citizen exchanges, Perez approached AAM, which was also considering how to keep IPAM relevant for twenty-first-century museums. But AAM officers were reluctant to risk relinquishing their current funding levels (IPAM garnered them

$350,000 per year), and DOS had to push them to engage in a larger conversation about the nature of their flagship international initiative.

AAM's eventual decision to rethink IPAM also arose from a desire to operate a program that would help U.S. museums work with their communities more broadly than IPAM's individual people-to-people initiative could. Heather Berry, manager of international programs, explained:

> The IPAM program didn't really meet the needs of the museums here in the U.S. and abroad because they were doing these great projects and yet no one in their community knew about it. And of course one of our main goals here at AAM is to advocate for museums locally and to make sure their communities understand what an important role they play in education, in bringing tourists locally, and it just wasn't giving the museums enough to share more broadly with their community.[70]

IPAM participants also recognized this limitation. During the last IPAM cycle (2005–7) Mark Heppner, the vice president of the museum services division and a curator at Stan Hywet Hall and Gardens in Akron, Ohio, undertook a partnership with Patoo Cusripituck from the National Discovery Museum Institute in Bangkok, Thailand. They set out to explore the history of both countries' rubber industries and the linked political and social effects. The planned traveling exhibition and book did not materialize because both the individuals and the project lacked deep institutional dedication from their museums. Heppner remembered his IPAM experience fondly, describing it nearly ten years later as "life changing," but recalled that the isolation of the museum professionals engaged in the program was a significant problem: "I got the blessing to go [to Thailand] but my colleagues, my supervisor, nobody really understood what this was, even though I did a presentation before I went and when I came back. But I don't know if there was really appreciation or fully understanding the perks of this."[71] He suggested that this lack of wider support prevented his project from ever reaching its full potential or producing intended outcomes.

In addition to issues related to the breadth of IPAM's impact, financial considerations were also at play. As the cost of living rose with global inflation between 1980 and 2007, fewer projects could be funded as AAM and DOS attempted to meet the evolving financial needs of program participants. In July 2006 Kim Igoe, the director of international programs at AAM, wrote to Perez and pointedly addressed these concerns: "After our meeting I formed a team within AAM to imagine a new kind of international partnership program that would be flexible, focused on outcomes, demonstrate an impact in a perceptible timeframe, and have a greater impact on communities in the US and abroad."[72] Berry later recalled that there was a similarity between the two organizations' desires for the new program and that "greater impact on communities" reflected, from AAM's perspective, a desire to help U.S. museums engage in more significant ways with their communities and locales.[73]

While both DOS and AAM wanted a more efficient program with a larger impact, the underlying assumptions of public diplomacy and public history were creating an unresolved tension about how to position power while connecting people and engaging in discussion. People-to-people public diplomacy may be based on exchange and dialogue, but it is motivated by the desire to improve U.S. standing in the world and boost the nation's power. In contrast, the evolving paradigm of public history, while not uniformly embraced, has adopted the notion of sharing authority: a mantra that assumes that the public historian has the authority to share but is focusing that sharing on audiences and stakeholders. The outcome of this is not to convince or influence, as in people-to-people diplomacy, but to engage in collaborative meaning making. Thus, from the beginning, these two intended outcomes were thus built into the new program known as MCCA.

These were not the only incongruities built into MCCA. The growth of the Internet and its ability to break down national and international boundaries had changed how DOS was targeting new international audiences through public diplomacy. Using both "tough-" and "tender-minded" approaches, post-9/11 programs were designed to engage young populations and minority groups—including indigenous populations—who had been ignored by previous public diplomacy efforts but were beginning to use the Internet to construct a political voice. As Perez explained, "our public diplomacy [after the Cold War] was focused on elites and decision makers and opinion shapers," but these new targeted populations "are not traditional pin-stripe suit decision makers. We need to refocus."[74] Yet including these audiences, especially young people, as project participants meant that museums had to navigate additional hierarchies in their community collaborations.

A white paper created by AAM and presented to DOS ECA proposed three possible new programs. Community engagement was at the center of each program's proposed mission statements. Each proposal clearly reflected the trend of museums engaging with their communities while expanding the reach and public diplomacy of the program. One option, named International Action Grants, was designed to "leverage the skills and expertise of US and non-US museum professionals and address specific problems or seize specific opportunities in communities." Another concept, IPAM 2.0, intended to "provide US museums and museums abroad with the resources needed to develop a community-centered international partnership with tangible outputs and demonstrated outcomes." The third, Museums and Community Collaborations Abroad, was designed to "build lasting ties between cultures; strengthen the connections between museums and their local communities; and create tools, models, and practices with the potential for widespread adoption."[75]

MCCA was chosen to succeed IPAM. As Berry recalled, "the first year it started [it] was also funded at $350,000, but they [DOS officials] were so excited about it that they then gave us an additional $100,000."[76] After some initial transition costs and a renaming of the program to Museums Connect in 2011, the program consistently funded between six and eight grants per year, each totaling between $50,000 and $100,000, with a 50 percent mandatory cost share by the U.S. museums. Perez explained this method of grant-making:

> We [DOS] work a lot with partners and one of the things that is really important to any kind of State Department funding is a transparent, competitive process. To run [Museums Connect] internally by the State Department would have taken us a lot of staff time and it would have required expertise that quite frankly we didn't have . . . [S]tructurally the Bureau of Educational and Cultural Affairs functions primarily through grant-making to partner organizations and that grant-making is always on a very open, competitive basis . . . Our whole cultural team might have been eight people to do all the cultural stuff we were trying to do: dance and music and everything else. I mean, there's no way [we could do it without partners].[77]

The discussions to shift from IPAM to MCCA thus emerged from the immediate context of financial efficiency and a movement toward more concrete ways to measure project outcomes that addressed both partners' needs. From the vantage point of AAM, the reimagining of its international program fit within the larger trend of museums moving toward direct engagement with their communities. From the DOS perspective, MCCA gave it the opportunity to engage more directly with communities and target audiences, especially young people. However, the similarities between people-to-people diplomacy and dialogic public history are limited, and the different intended outcomes—influencing non-U.S. publics and engaging in collaborative public history practices—formed the paradigm within which Museums Connect projects have operated since 2008.

"A COMPLEX GAME OF 'MULTIDIMENSIONAL CHESS'"

"Hip-hop is America," claimed then secretary of state, Hillary Clinton, in an interview on *CBS News* in 2010. Referring to a current DOS program that was sending U.S. Muslim rap artists to the Muslim world to counter negative perceptions of the United States, she argued that "we have to use every tool at our disposal."[78] Whether hip-hop, like jazz during DOS tours in the 1950s, "is America" is debatable.[79] Indeed, the counter-cultural origins of both musical genres are highlighted by Hishaam Aidi, who argues that the use of jazz in conveying "a sense of shared suffering, as well as the conviction that equality could be gained under the American political system" mirrored hip-hop's history as "outsiders' protest" against political systems in the United States, an attitude that now resonates among marginalized Muslim youth worldwide.[80] Yet the underlying sentiment of Clinton's argument highlights a broader understanding of the ideological assumptions underpinning public diplomacy that began during World War II. "You have to bet at the end of the day, people will choose freedom over tyranny if they're given a choice," she went on to say. Her argument was predicated on the idea that "cultural diplomacy is a complex game of 'multidimensional chess.'"[81] It also reflected a belief that engaging non-U.S. citizens in discussions about the United States, its culture, and its people (some of the pieces in this game of chess), and not just traditional diplomats in governmental diplomatic programs, will change their opinion of and behavior toward the nation. Clinton and others hoped that this would ease the development of official relationships and "enhance our national security in subtle, wide-ranging, and sustainable ways."[82] The approach still appears to be in sync with the practice of U.S. museums and public history more broadly: to engage wider audiences in their work, seek dialogue, and operate within a sphere of a shared authority. Nonetheless, from the beginning, Museums Connect was marked by the convergence of two paradigms: public history's interest in shared authority and public diplomacy's people-to-people diplomacy. Those different goals had a considerable effect on the program's implementation, activities, and achievements.[83]

CHAPTER 2

"Afghan on top and American on bottom"

Exploring Minority Identity through Dialogue with War-Torn Afghanistan

In the spring of 2010 a museum professional named Jeffrey Stern traveled to Afghanistan with his colleague Sayeh Hormozi to deliver, install, and formally unveil a photography exhibition titled *Being We the People*. The exhibition was the product of a one-year Museums Connect grant between the National Museum of Afghanistan (NMA) and Marefat High School in Kabul and the National Constitution Center (NCC) and Constitution High School in Philadelphia, Pennsylvania. Opening simultaneously at both museums, the exhibit was organized into sets of paired photographs, one taken by an Afghan student, one by an American student, with both captioned in English and Farsi. This format encouraged viewers to consider similarities and differences between the two photographs. At the Kabul opening, Stern was asked to share some remarks, which he subsequently described as "little" and only a small part of a larger ceremony. Yet his presence added the weight of the National Constitution Center and the U.S. side of the partnership to the event. The occasion's significance was not lost on Afghan media. Dozens of television and radio reporters, including representatives of

BBC Persia, attended, as did three hundred dignitaries and other guests.[1] The students at Marefat High School also understood the importance of the event. Marefat is a large school in western Kabul, and it educates Hazara children, members of an ethnic group that has been a historically persecuted minority in a majority Pashtun country. During the past century, the Hazara people have suffered not only terrible physical violence but also attempts at cultural genocide. The presence of their photographs in a national museum that symbolizes the ruling Pashtun majority and Hazara neglect gave this moment an added poignancy.

The symbolism of the opening extended further when one of the Marefat students suggested that Stern should wear a traditional Afghan outfit, the *shalwar kameez,* while giving his remarks. But Stern had little time to change clothes before the program began and ended up wearing the Afghan shirt—"sort of like a long pajama top"—over his American jeans. With a rueful laugh, he recalled that his eclectic outfit delighted the students, who suggested that, like the exhibition itself, he was "Afghan on top and American on bottom."[2]

The students' observation reflected the aesthetic decision of the exhibition's designers, who chose to place the Afghan photographs above the American photographs in the display. It also symbolized the power dynamics of the project as a whole. The NCC, like other U.S. lead museums involved in Museums Connect projects, possessed significantly more professional skill and expertise (at least according to western scholarship definitions) than NMA did. While the NMA provided exhibition space, it otherwise had little involvement in the day-to-day operations of the project and the exhibition's development. Yet Stern, as the project director, created conditions for the project that positioned him and his NCC colleagues as facilitators rather than knowledge givers.[3] Moreover, the choice of photography as an exhibition medium, inspired by the Hazara photographer Nasim Fekrat (a friend of Stern's), as well as the selection of comparable schools to act as community partners, allowed *Being We the People* to realize a dialogic mode of public history in which two groups of students engaged in a shared and self-guided exploration of the project's theme within the parameters laid out by NCC facilitators.[4] Marefat students were able negotiate their ethnic minority identity at home (at the symbolically important National Museum of Afghanistan) as well as abroad (during their trip to Philadelphia).

The NCC staff's interpretation of the grant theme was different from what appeared in the original proposal. They focused on the title of the project, *Being We the People*, and the pluralist ideas embedded within the phrase, while marginalizing the original idea laid out in the project's original goals and suggested in its subtitle: *Afghanistan, America & the Minority Imprint*.[5] This had the effect of effacing the "minority imprint" of the Philadelphia students and promoting contemporary comparisons between the two countries rather than nuanced discussions about the histories of the two minority groups in Philadelphia and Kabul and how they had influenced the present circumstances of their communities.

"PREACHING TO THE CHOIR": THE PROJECT AND THE PARTNERS

The NCC in Philadelphia approaches the study of the past through dialogue strategies born of the ideological positions embedded within the U.S. Constitution, particularly a broadly celebratory idea of pluralism. The center was established during the early years of the culture wars, when political conservatives feared that the nation's history and founding principles were being overlooked or replaced by new revisionist histories that denigrated America's past. A strict patriotic orthodoxy emerged that "embraced a past which, its proponents claimed, had only one true and unchanging meaning."[6] President Ronald Reagan's signature on the Constitution Heritage Act of 1988 called for a continuation of the Constitution's 1987 bicentennial celebration through the creation of "a national center 'within or in close proximity to the Independence National Historical Park' that 'shall disseminate information about the United States Constitution on a nonpartisan basis in order to increase awareness and understanding of the Constitution among the American people.'" Opened on July 4, 2003, the center—a private, nonprofit organization—became an example of the new paradigm of U.S. museums, one that focused on discussion and dialogue and decentered the authority of traditional collections of artifacts and the power of an authoritative interpretive voice. Through interactive exhibitions, conversations, public forums, and public programming, it works to fulfill its patriotic mission "to illuminate constitutional ideals and inspire active citizenship."[7] Although this approach appears to contradict the founding legislation that required the "dissemination of information," the NCC's commitment to hosting forums, presidential debates, and other dialogues on contemporary issues in U.S. public life reflects the late-twentieth-century view that museum visitors learn best when engaging in dialogue and knowledge creation rather than passively consuming a master narrative dictated by an exhibition's curator.

The NCC's goals of civic education and the development of an active citizenry, especially among young people, led it to open Constitution High School in 2006. The school is a Philadelphia public school with 93 percent minority enrollment. Under the motto "Law, Democracy, and History," the school's curriculum centers around Philadelphia's history as the symbolic center of U.S. democracy. Its website publicly promises that "[b]y engaging students with an appreciation for history and an understanding of the democratic principles embodied in the United States Constitution, this college preparatory high school will develop the next generation of engaged citizens and civic leaders in government, public policy, and law."[8]

The principles of civic discourse that guide both NCC and Constitution High School also inspired Joe Torsella, a former NCC chief executive, and Hugh Allen, the center's senior director of special projects and government relations, when they began the international program at NCC in 2007. The goals were to extend the museum's reach beyond its stated domestic mission and create dialogue with populations beyond U.S. national boundaries, especially in so-called emerging democracies. "What we do at the museum is really special and it's really important," Allen said. "And this is probably the type of thing that we should look to do when we do international work." He believed that expanding NCC's model by acting as a space for dialogue among different groups across international boundaries would extend the center's guiding strategy for domestic work into an international context.[9] However, because NCC frames dialogue within the context of furthering understanding of the Constitution, he focused on creating an international program that would promote such ideas abroad.

Allen's decision to hire Jeff Stern, then working as a journalist, rather than a traditionally trained museum professional to run NCC's international program unexpectedly challenged NCC institutional ideology when it began its Museums Connect project in 2009. Prior to joining NCC, Stern worked at the American University of Afghanistan in Kabul, where his boss was an Afghan—a situation he described as unusual for most U.S. citizens working in the country. Through a partnership with the university, he began teaching English at Marefat High School. In the beginning he knew nothing about the school or its ethnic Hazara students but, however raw his instruction, found himself learning a great deal about the Hazara and developing close friendships and sympathies with its faculty and students. Throughout his time in Afghanistan he also became cynical about governmental and nongovernmental aid and development projects that, he felt, "preach[ed] U.S. values" and stood in opposition to his journalistic urge to "professionally criticiz[e] the U.S. approach to Afghanistan." These relationships and this context became significant when he was hired by NCC to develop international programs with a focus on post-conflict nations. At first he worked on a number of small projects with Marefat students and faculty, including creating a voting guide in Afghanistan. So when the Museums Connect request for proposals was sent out from AAM in 2008, he believed "it was very obvious that the Marefat School would be the perfect one."[10]

Marefat High School was founded in exile in Pakistan after the civil war began in Afghanistan in 1994. By the end of 2001, it had opened six coeducational branches in the Rawalpindi-Islamabad region as well as in Attock and Peshawar. After the fall of the Taliban in Afghanistan in 2002, five branches of the school were moved to Kabul, and the main branch ceased operation in Pakistan in 2006. In Kabul Marefat was consolidated into one property in the mostly Hazara-occupied slums of Dasht-e-Barchi in the western section of the city. The school educated thousands of Hazara students, including a high percentage of girls, using a curriculum that was unique within Afghanistan. It received financial support from Baroness Dr. Frances D'Souza, the former speaker of the British House of Lords. While most schools in the country emphasize rote memorization and basic literacy, Marefat proudly describes its approach as "[p]roductive civic and democratic subjects in the curriculum: Humanism, Human Rights, Democracy."[11]

In 2004, Hamid Karzai's government instituted changes in Afghanistan and created the country's constitution; and in 2005 the Hazara school gave up its coeducational status by order of the Ministry of Education. When students protested the 2009 Shia family law that restricted women's rights, the school came under attack from conservative clerics and their supporters and was banned from teaching civics in 2012.[12] Nonetheless, the school continues to maintain a progressive focus that it describes as "[e]ducative civic and democratic practices, such as students elected representatives in the Board of Trustees, students' parliament, students' class councils."[13] Under the leadership of Azizullah Royesh—who was nominated as a finalist for the 2014 Global Teacher Award and has served as a Yale World Fellow—Marefat's progressive curriculum and its focus on civic education mirrored the focus of its U.S. partners.[14] Moreover, persecution by the Taliban and other ethnic groups made the Hazaras and their school receptive to the United States and the wider international community. Thus, when Stern approached Royesh about partnering on a Museums Connect project, he quickly agreed. While planning and writing the Museums Connect grant, Stern speculated that, had he approached any other institution in Afghanistan to partner with NMA, NCC, and Constitution High School, there may have been a clash of values or intentions. Thanks to his relationship with Marefat, this "lucky" partnership could be planned between stakeholders who "were just so aligned."[15]

Being We the People (officially titled *We, the People: Afghanistan, America, and the Minority Imprint*) was designed by Stern, Allen, and the photographer Nasim Fekrat as a collaborative exploration of the lives of minority students at Constitution High School and Marefat School. The goal would be a student photography exhibition opening simultaneously at NMA and NCC at the end of the one-year project (2009–10). Originally, the organizers planned to unfold the project digitally through Skype workshops and Shutterfly.com discussions, and four NCC staff members were slated to travel to Kabul to develop it and lend support and technical expertise to NMA.[16] In addition, "[a]fter the photographs, videos, and oral histories are collected and critiqued, students, teachers, and museum staff from Marefat High School and the National Museum of Afghanistan will travel to the United States for the design and installation of the final exhibition, which will open in May 2010."[17]

In 2011, as he reflected on NCC's subsequent Museums Connect project with the Natural History Museum of Latvia, Allen described his institution's approach vis-à-vis international programs: "[Y]ou bring people together and then you do what museums do: you bring people together and then you get the hell out of the way."[18] Stern took a similar approach in guiding decision-making and constructing the conditions under which the Philadelphia and Kabul students would engage in a shared exploration of their ideas. His prior experience as an aid worker and journalist in Afghanistan undoubtedly shaped the form and function of NCC's international work. With his deep connections to the Hazara, he was able to create conditions for *Being We the People* that elevated the role of students in both countries and allowed them to act together as "public curators."[19] Royesh confirmed these dynamics when he recalled that the project functioned as "a joint venture program through which the students found some brilliant peers at the Constitution High School. They shot many scenes that helped them ponder on the roots and richness of their country's culture and customs."[20]

Because Stern was eager to develop a project that was different from what he perceived as traditional, U.S.-controlled, neocolonial programs in Afghanistan, he embraced Fekrat's idea for the structure of *Being We the People*.[21] In early 2008 Fekrat had traveled around Afghanistan, and he later recalled that his fellow countrymen did not identify him as Afghan. "People didn't recognize me, they called me Chinese."[22] This experience was not unique to Fekrat but was common in the country, where the Hazara have been marginalized and persecuted because they are largely Shiite in a majority Sunni country. They also look different from the other ethnic groups in Afghanistan. In a 2008 *National Geographic* feature, Phil Zabriskie described them as having "Asian features—narrow eyes, flat noses, broad cheeks—[that] set them apart in a de facto lower class."[23] Frustrated by the lack of Hazara media representation and fearing their larger marginalization, Fekrat speculated that a mobile exhibition that highlighted all of the country's ethnic groups could "introduce Afghans to Afghans in order to bring all Afghans together."[24] This fledgling idea, conveyed informally between friends, became the foundational activity of *Being We the People* and was expanded to include the notion of pairing

Afghan with U.S. students after the call-for-proposals for Museums Connect crossed Stern's desk at NCC.

Without prompting, Royesh confirmed the importance of Stern's leadership and the conditions that he created for the project: "The most important element of the success was Jeff Stern and his wonderful management of everything. He was a marvelous engine of the project."[25] Stern saw the museum's role as facilitator rather than knowledge giver. As his colleague Sayeh Hormozi, NCC's senior manager of civic and international engagement, reflected, "We really were just facilitating their work, we gave them so much ownership of the project, [we] were there to just support them and facilitate their vision for the partnership with the students." As an example, she cited providing transport to take the U.S. students to different locations around Philadelphia, including polling places during the 2008 U.S. presidential election, and noted that the students directed the photography process rather than the NCC staff.[26] For his part, Royesh recalled how *Being We the People* fit into Marefat's civic engagement curriculum: "[Marefat students] could turn the page and have their imprint. For me, this was the practical aspect of my theories shared with the students in my civic education classes. I would try to help them be the citizens of their country. Now, they could show their reach . . . Now I could see that dream realized and that mission accomplished. That would [later] give me a pleasing sense of relief and content."[27] The two schools' focus on civic education was compatible with the mission of the NCC, and this precondition allowed the student participants to engage in a shared exploration through dialogue, as did Stern's prior relationship with Marefat High School and the Hazara and his unwillingness to proclaim U.S. virtues abroad (although this was contrary to NCC's ideological position and the fundamental ideas underpinning people-to-people diplomacy). As a result, NCC staff embraced the paradigm of museum professionals as facilitators who would enable the students' work.[28]

"[A] NATION STAYS ALIVE WHEN ITS CULTURE STAYS ALIVE"

NCC's museum partner in Afghanistan, the NMA, was significantly less involved in the project than the two schools were, and the U.S.-weighted power dynamics embedded in Museums Connect became even more pronounced due to significant differences between the functions and capacities of the partnering institutions. Although several provincial museums have existed in Afghanistan during the past one hundred years, including ones in Jalalabad, Herat, and Ghazni, the NMA is the largest and has been the most consistently operated. It opened as the Kabul Museum in 1919, amid a wave of anticolonial sentiment after the British relinquished control of the country. Its early collections included "manuscripts, miniatures, weapons and art objects belonging to the former royal families." In 1931 it relocated from Bagh-e-Bala Palace to its present location in southwestern Kabul. In 1965 it was renamed the National Museum of Afghanistan.[29]

Like many European and U.S. museums founded in the same era, the NMA has devoted much of the past seventy-five years to preserving its nation's antiquities. In Afghanistan many of these were discovered during the excavation of sites along the Silk Road.[30] Through agreements and partnerships with international archaeologists the NMA accumulated a significant collection of art, paintings, sculpture, coins, jewelry, and other ancient artifacts from across the country during the first half of the twentieth century. According to the museum's official history, "[t]he original collection was dramatically enriched, beginning in 1922, by the first excavations of the Délégation Archéologique Française en Afghanistan (DAFA). Through the years other archaeological delegations have added their finds to the museum until today the collection spans fifty millenniums Prehistoric, Classical, Buddhist, Hindu and Islamic and stands as one of the greatest testimonies of antiquity that the world has inherited."[31]

According to the scholar Nancy Dupree, "[b]y the 1970s . . . the [NMA] displays presented a remarkably complete visual record of the cultural history of the Afghan area for 100,000 years, from the prehistoric to the ethnographic present, and, since the objects were excavated from Afghan soil, the collections truly represented the cultural heritage of all Afghan peoples."[32] Yet she lamented that before the Soviet invasion and the "assault on culture" in the 1970s, the museum—like many in southern Asia—did not effectively serve the people of Afghanistan, play a significant role in public life, or contribute to a sense of "nation."[33] Her critique reflected her U.S. upbringing and her view of U.S. museums as central repositories of national memory: "[H]eritage subjects were not included in any meaningful way in the school curriculum. School children were rarely taught about the richness of their past; field trips to museums or historical sites were not part of school activities. Few mature adults ever visited the museum."[34]

Yet Afghanistan's context for the production of historical knowledge and memory is significantly different from the U.S. one, especially given its recent history of war and trauma. It is continuously constructed, revised, and revisited in the active memory work of its citizens rather than on the walls or in the cases of the NMA. The anthropologist Parin Dossa has noted that quotidian storytelling in Afghanistan, especially by women, connects the past to the present and serves as a teaching tool for the country's children. It "does not merely evoke the past; it impacts the present."[35]

Since the early 1970s, political turbulence has had a significant effect on the NMA and other public history sites across the country, further diminishing public engagement with these institutions and their wider relevance. Violence during the overthrow of King Mohammed Zahir Shah in 1973, the military coup of April 1978, the 1979 Soviet invasion, the Taliban takeover following the retreat of the Soviets in 1989, and a civil war in the 1990s damaged and destroyed much of Afghanistan's cultural heritage at the NMA and other sites around the country. Looting and theft and the deliberate removal and destruction of Buddhist and other early artifacts that countered the Taliban's narrative about Afghanistan's history and religious and cultural heritage crippled the institution, which was left struggling to conduct basic operations. Damage to the museum extended to its staff, many of whom were arrested, mistreated, or killed for trying to preserve the country's historical and cultural heritage.

Omara Khan Massoudi, the director of the NMA since 2001 and an employee at the museum since 1978, summarized the situation as "the destruction of the economy and the cultural infrastructure."[36] Predicting that the Mujahideen's rise to power could be disastrous for the museum, he and his skeleton staff attempted to hide some of the most valuable artifacts, including the newly excavated Bactrian treasures, in a number of vaults around Kabul, including the Central Bank and the Presidential

Palace. These actions were prescient: the NMA, along with archeological sites, other museums, and government agencies, were plundered during the civil war that followed the resignation of Communist president Mohammad Najibullah in 1992. Then, on March 12, 1994, the museum, which was being used as a military base and defensive position, was struck by a rocket and damaged. By 1996, 70 percent of the collection had been looted. And after 2001, when the Taliban leader Mullah Omar "issued an edict" sponsoring widespread iconoclasm to rewrite the country's pre-Islamic history, roughly 2,500 works of art, sculpture, and artifacts at the NMA as well as the Bamiyan Buddhas in the Hazarajat region were destroyed or defaced.[37]

These actions sparked international outrage, and many organizations, including UNESCO, responded by working to protect the NMA's building and collection—sometimes successfully, sometimes not. In 1994 Dupree and other concerned individuals founded the Society for the Preservation of Afghanistan's Cultural Heritage (SPACH) in Islamabad, with the goal of recovering as much of the country's national history as possible.[38] In that same year Sotirios Mousouris, representing the U.N. secretary general and the U.N. Office for the Coordination of Humanitarian Affairs (UNOCHA), visited Afghanistan to offer dedicated assistance to NMA to support its basic functioning and its work to protect its collection from destruction. International support has since become a central funding stream, as Afghanistan's government investment has vacillated over time.

International partnerships and support were also central to the NMA's work after the Taliban was overthrown in 2001. Alongside museum staff, visiting conservators and technicians restored, catalogued, and preserved the parts of the collection that had remained in Kabul.[39] In the spirit of the museum's unofficial motto, "[a] nation stays alive when its culture stays alive," DOS, the National Endowment for the Humanities, and other agencies and organizations pledged financial and material support to help preserve Afghanistan's cultural heritage.[40] Cultural heritage professionals William Remsen and Laura Tedesco point out that, aside from a brief interlude in the 1990s, when DOS cultural diplomacy budgets were reduced, "the US government has long recognized the value of cultural diplomacy and the preservation of Afghanistan's endangered cultural patrimony for the present and future generations of the Afghan nation and the world." They continue: "Afghan cultural heritage preservation and development are integral parts of larger US public diplomacy efforts to support Afghanistan's people and government as they establish a more secure, prosperous and resilient state."[41]

After 2001, both Afghanistan's transitional government and outside observers hoped that the NMA and the country's larger public history would assume a more central position in Afghan public life. As Dupree wrote in 2002, "the global interest in Afghanistan presents unique opportunities" in this regard. In 2004 the transitional government passed the Law on the Preservation of Historical and Cultural Heritage, reflecting de jure attempts to protect the country's historical and cultural heritage. The 2011 announcement of a government plan to rebuild the NMA was another positive move. Yet national history continues to be invisible in most school curricula, and the NMA continues to occupy a symbolic role that serves tourists rather than the Afghan people, making it clear that notions about the nation are fledgling, fragmented, and divisive and that memory practices are not focused around national museums or modes of public history production and dissemination as they are in the United States and Europe. Since 2001, this has been reinforced by the prioritization of government functions in the process of nation building, which has left the NMA poorly funded.[42]

Public disagreements about the nation's history have also diminished the importance of the recent past in official national narratives. A debate about the version of history that appeared in the country's post-2002 textbooks proved so divisive that they now no longer cover national history after 1973. Farooq Wardak, the former education minister, explained, "Our recent history tears us apart. We've created a curriculum based on the older history that brings us together, with figures universally recognized as being great." Any discussion of history in the public sphere is a positive development, and history as it is being taught in schools is intended to "encourage brotherhood and unity." The problem, according to Wardak, is that the recent past is not widely seen as important to the new nation. Thus, as Remsen and Tedesco have noted, "Two generations of young Afghans, who have grown up with war or outside their own country as refugees, have little idea about their remarkable cultural past." This sentiment emerged in interviews I conducted with members of the

Museums Connect project team and others familiar with the NMA. Fekrat said, "Museums here [in the United States] are for education and you go in, [but] in Afghanistan that is not how they are viewed." A project participant named Azam mirrored criticisms of museums in other countries when he suggested that the historical narratives of the museum served the ruling elites but had little relevance to the lives of everyday citizens: "It [NMA] is a very formal, decorative projection of the history. All of these words of kings, or, for example, the pottery of the kingdom or the crowns of the kings, and there is little of culture in it and little of civilization in it. It doesn't mean that there [wasn't] anything to display but it's because it was how they [the ruling elites] wanted it to be, a very formal description of the history they wanted and liked."[43] This view is also supported by Constance Wyndham's analysis of NMA as a site that features an abundance of Buddhist statues in a central location and relegates and diminishes the Islamic pieces, which are relevant to the nation's overwhelmingly Muslim population, to the physical and intellectual periphery.[44]

In spite of such challenges, Hamid Karzai's government used the NMA enthusiastically as a vehicle for international affairs. The recovered artifacts from vaults around Kabul, including the Bactrian treasures—21,000 pieces of gold jewelry and artifacts dating to the first century BCE—formed an international traveling exhibition, *Afghanistan: Hidden Treasures from the National Museum,* in 2006. This exhibition was created with support from the National Geographic Society and traveled to major museums in Europe, Australia, and the United States to showcase a "different side" of Afghanistan to the world.[45] In the exhibition's catalogue, Omar Sultan, the former deputy minister of information and culture, explained, "By organizing this exhibition, we want to affirm our commitment to the international community that Afghanistan is changing from a culture of war to a culture of peace." He declared that the Ministry of Information, Culture, Tourism, and Youth was committed to encouraging a new atmosphere of peace "through cultural gatherings, cultural heritage events, and festivals," with the goal of "lift[ing] people's spirits but also . . . promoting a culture of tolerance and understanding."[46] The exhibition's overtly political and diplomatic context was confirmed by Karzai's introductory letter, which was printed in the exhibition's North

American catalogue: "When I was elected President of Afghanistan, one of my promises to the Afghan people was that the world would never forget our country. 'Hidden Treasures' will paint a panoramic picture of our wondrous country and let the beauty of Afghanistan come alive in the imaginations of our friends around the world." In a 2013 interview Massoudi concurred, optimistically suggesting that NMA could play a significant role in "introduc[ing] the other face of Afghanistan to people" around the world.[47]

Given these outward-facing sentiments, the NMA embraced the Museums Connect project when the U.S. embassy in Kabul approached it as a possible partner. Hugh Allen recalled that Massoudi "was fully willing. He signed . . . the concept papers and was like 'Yes, this is great, this is wonderful recognition for their museum, and wonderful recognition for the country to be involved with the U.S. State Department.'" But the practical limitations of expertise and resources at an institution that lacked reliable electrical power and was trying to recover from decades of damage meant that NMA's role would be limited to serving primarily as an exhibition space. Its community partner, Marefat High School, conducted the day-to-day project activities and developed the exhibition. Massoudi later acknowledged that "interaction with the National Constitution Center mainly happened through Marefat High School. We rarely contacted them."[48]

BEING WE THE PEOPLE

The students in Philadelphia and Kabul approached the project's central ideas and themes from widely disparate public history contexts (via the U.S. Constitution and fraught current events), and as a result each group interpreted the phrase "Being We the People" very differently. Because of these discrepancies in interpretation, the student photographers moved the project beyond its original goal of a study of the histories of the two minority communities and their imprint toward a comparative look at the groups' contemporary similarities and differences. Participants' lack of consensus about the phrase's meaning highlights the folly of assuming that every person uniformly understood the intentions or stated goals of the project creators at NCC, demonstrating the importance of considering project participants both collectively and individually.

The opening phrase of the preamble to the U.S. Constitution holds significant popular meaning in the United States and, for many, immediately evokes considerations of the political power placed in the hands of the people and their elected officials. The constitutional scholar Bruce Ackerman argues that the idea of government by the people remains both a central idea and a distinctive feature of the Constitution. While the notion originated in the United States, it is not totally restricted to the United States. For instance, after the Bonn Agreement of December 2001, which required the new state of Afghanistan to rewrite its constitution, the country ratified a new constitution in 2004 that included the phrase "We the People" in its preamble.[49]

The U.S. and Afghan constitutions were not the only sources for the Museums Connect project's theme and guiding ideas. It was also framed using key themes from the U.N.'s Universal Declaration of Human Rights "such as work, religion, participation, expression, commerce, and myself." Together these documents guided Stern and NCC's choice of the project theme. At NCC the phrase "We the People," U.S. constitutional ideals, and celebratory ideas of pluralism were not abstract concepts but central elements of the museum's mission. In fact, one of the permanent exhibitions is titled *The Story of We the People*. Thus, the initial goals of the *Being We the People* project reinforced a deep institutional ideology, which shaped the NCC staff's perspectives and influenced how they framed the project to the Constitution High School students.[50]

Lauren Cristella, NCC's education manager, spoke of the process of creating the original year-long project curriculum:

> "Being We the People" is taking the ideas, specifically from the preamble but beyond that this whole "Great American Experiment" and everything that entails, and saying, "What does that look like day to day? What does that look like for a high school student here?" And by the same principles, we [the U.S. government] were helping Afghanistan write their constitution, they were just coming out of the constitution-writing process for Afghanistan, [and] what does that mean? And this is the manifestation of that, through photography.[51]

Cristella's description revealed NCC's expectations about the kinds of subjects the students' photographs might document in order to frame the project as a unifying and homogeneous "us" and "them." Not only did this expectation efface the grant proposal's original goal of exploring "the minority imprint," but it also assumed that both groups of students would interpret the project's theme in the same way: that the centrality of ideas embedded in the U.S. Constitution would be mirrored in Afghanistan. In other words, it aligned with people-to-people diplomacy's pursuit of similarities rather than dissonance. Cristella recalled that she and her colleagues hoped that both groups of students "would glean an understanding of how similar their societies are. I think their gut reaction was that it's so different, it's a war zone, they don't believe what we believe, and it's a world away. It just seemed so far away; a lot of our students had never left Philadelphia."[52] Such attitudes overlooked the participants' diverse experiences of both citizenship and minority status. By reflecting traditional celebratory notions of pluralism, it promoted the teenagers' similarities rather than interrogating their challenges. One of NCC's earliest blog posts about *Being We the People* agreed with Cristella's interpretation of the project's goals: "One can expect [each group's] photographs and interpretations of freedom to vastly differ from one another. However, perhaps what the resulting exhibition will actually show us is how similar these young people really are despite the thousands of miles and years of life experiences that separate them."[53]

Stern, too, hoped the grant would draw comparisons between the two countries rather than between the two minority populations:

> I think that the American students from the Afghan students and the Afghan students from the American students got something that is unique to photography, which is if you're in a class and you're looking at an image, and it's just an image and it's not a video, and it's not a story, you are compelled to focus on one thing. An Afghan student can present a part of their world to an American student that is difficult—not impossible—but difficult to do with another medium. Because there is nothing else competing for your attention. There is a single, stark image. And you have a discussion about one image.[54]

Yet such interpretations of the project marginalized the minority experiences of the Constitution High School students (the school has 93 percent minority enrollment compared to Pennsylvania's state average of 32 percent) and promoted a comparative frame instead.[55] This was exacerbated by the NCC staff's tendency to elevate and celebrate the Marefat students' minority status as members of the Hazara ethnic group. Staff members demonstrated great admiration, sympathy, and respect for those students and their school, suggesting that they deserved particular reverence and respect for what they had been able to achieve in the face of persecution. This had the effect of diminishing the minority status of the Philadelphia students, who were seen and treated as privileged U.S. citizens vis-à-vis their less privileged Afghan colleagues. Allen's description of the partnership reflected this subtle attitude, one that also permeated other NCC staff members' recollections:

> And what was unique about that [the project] was that the students that we worked with in both schools were predominantly minorities. Most of our students in Philadelphia were African American and most of our students in Afghanistan were Hazara. And Hazaras are a very distinct and very many times persecuted minority in Afghanistan. You know, African Americans have come a long way in the United States and there are certainly still issues, but [they are] nowhere near as persecuted as Hazaras are.[56]

Hormozi's stratification of the two minority groups' relative tragedies was less overt than Allen's was. Yet even though she suggested that the groups could bond over their shared minority status, she relegated the African American community to second place:

> [One piece] for the American students, I think, [was] knowing who was coming, having this advanced time to think and prepare and understand who was coming to visit them and what they [the Marefat students] had been through. And I think the other piece of it was that our students that we worked with and the school that we worked with were largely an African American population and this was a school that was a majority-minority school. And there also—[in] the African American community—there are always these questions about marginalization and [they] have this history of persecution and being marginalized that they are continuing to strive against today, and here we have these Hazara students who have that similar threat and background, and I think that was a connection that our students made. That these are students who have also experienced some of the ethnic and racial bigotry that they've experienced. I think thinking about them in terms of people to

> be compassionate toward because of the war and all the atrocities that they have gone through.[57]

As a result of such attitudes, activities conducted early in the project diminished the minority status of the Philadelphia students, framing them instead as representatives of the United States, in keeping with people-to-people diplomacy's reinforcement of the nation-state and national identity. Allen recalled, "One of the first things we asked the American students to write [was] what they would say to an Afghan audience if they were the United States government, and then we asked the Afghan students to essentially write their equivalent of the president's state of the union speech if he were speaking on the topic of their country. So we'd do things like that to get them warmed up, to get to know each other."[58]

Students recognized that NCC staff had, from the first, taken control of the project's framing and theme. Samantha, an African American student in Philadelphia, reflected that *Being We the People* "didn't mean anything until the end of the project. For me it was like an essay, we filled in all the words and the title at that point came to fruition." Only after the project was over did she see the title phrase as an inclusive term that "encompassed all of us all over the world." She continued: "I learned about the similarities between our worlds. I learned that they were and are fighting for the same rights and liberties we have and desire in America. They are very educated about world issues, and . . . the type of knowledge we received throughout our lifetime was quite different." Samantha's recollections, while revealing her embrace of the normative pluralist narrative of the United States and herself as an "American," also reflected a transnational sensibility that looked at rights and liberties beyond the lens of the nation-state. Likewise, Kayla, a Jamaican-born student at Constitution High School, said, "*Being We the People* reflects that no matter our cultural, ethnical, or racial background there are similar grounds that we walk on . . . [It] is turning our backs away from our own trivial concerns about life and focusing on bigger issues that affects human rights by taking a physical approach to inspire and make change."[59]

Both of these comments highlight an inclusive approach to the similarities between the students rather than a complex wrestling with their similarities and differences, which was how the project was originally framed. While Samantha showed an awareness of a transnational sensibility that moved beyond the nation-state frame, when pressed to consider the subtitle of the project, "the minority imprint," she said she didn't "think so much about it until we had to think about the context of our photos [while pairing them]. Some of my photos were of graffiti in alleyways and the oh-so-familiar teddy bear memorials at every street corner. At that point you can only do a root-cause analysis as to why that was the norm for me. While taking photos I really tried to just have fun."[60]

The meanings that the Constitution High School students derived from the project were reflected in the exhibition. For example, Dominiq Gilyard's photograph of a Philadelphia grocery store had this caption: "The market was so full of food, but empty of people. There are all kinds of high-grade meats, veal, pork, beef, but no one buying it. In Afghanistan, there are people looking for food, but there isn't as much as there is here, so it's the reverse of this photo. This represents how I feel we have a lot of stuff, and it is important for people to share." The photograph was paired with one of a Kabul shop by a Marefat student, Bismillah Alizada, which had a similar composition of neatly symmetrical rows of goods on sale. The caption read, "This is a shop in which different kinds of cooking ingredients like spices and oils are sold."[61] This pairing and the tone of the captions were representative of the larger exhibition, which defaulted to identifying similar visual and compositional aesthetics while collectively neglecting particular "minority imprints" in either country. In so doing, it offered a homogeneous vision of the United States and Afghanistan, regardless of the photographers' backgrounds, rather than a deeper look at specific historical, political, or social contexts.

The title *Being We the People: Afghanistan, America & the Minority Imprint* was much more carefully interrogated in Afghanistan because the project theme was less readily apparent, despite the linked terminology in the new constitution of Afghanistan. Fekrat guided the Marefat students as they embarked on the photography project: "The purpose was to document everyday life and project it to a different audience, while in the meantime learn about themselves."[62] Both Stern and Fekrat saw the camera as a tool through which students could look at their own lives, surroundings, and communities through a still, finite image. Royesh agreed, recalling that the students at his high school were able to see themselves in a new light through the process of creating photographs: "They shot many scenes that helped them ponder on the roots and richness of their country's culture and customs. They learned how to work in a group with a specific agenda and a visionary mission."[63] One Marefat student, Azam, said,

> Photography helped me to see the very tiny details of society that I often was not able to see with my eyes . . . Each of the times I was going to take these photos it opened the time for a short discussion about what they [the photograph's subjects] were doing, how their lives were, and what they were thinking about society, about government, about education, all of this stuff. I think that this was a very good experience. The pictures gave me the opportunity to go into the details of people's lives, of social interactions, of the tiny details of culture, and how people lived.[64]

Students in Kabul did not have to deal with the marginalization of their minority identity, as the Philadelphia students did. In Royesh's view, *Being We the People* "meant the importance of people in a democratic system. People are the ultimate source of authority and the last body to legitimize any decision related to their destiny and life." This theme and its underlying ideas connected intimately to the unique civic education that he was helping to lead at Marefat High School: "I looked at this phrase as the basis of my theory about civic education or civic awareness. It provided me with a context in which I could bring my students to explore and practice their own power as people. For my students, it simply implied the notion of people as the tangible figures around them. They identified themselves as 'being we the people.'" This theory was made manifest in the photographs that the students took. Royesh recalled that, from his perspective, "the people" of the project's theme came to mean not only the students but also the subjects of their photographs and, later, their partner students in Philadelphia.[65]

Royesh's contextual readings of the phrase "We the People" and the broader intellectual framework through which he considered its implications for the project were not commonly mirrored in other responses from Hazara facilitators and students. Those who were less familiar with the U.S. and Afghan constitutions did not call upon related ideas and theories regarding democratic participation. They understood the central idea of the project in different ways. Fekrat, for instance, did not know that the phrase appeared in the new Afghan constitution. Instead, he framed his understanding of the project's guiding concept within the ethnic identity of the Hazara. He explained that, in Afghanistan, individuals do not identify as "Afghan" (which he subversively said is often used derogatorily when directed at other ethnic groups, a way to imply lack of education or backwardness) but as members of their ethnic group. Thus, for him, "We the People" had no inherent meaning but "was interpreted as 'We the people of Hazara.'"[66] He saw this as empowering because it drew the focus of other Afghans and the Philadelphia project participants to a historically marginalized and little-seen group. While his interpretation diverged from understandings linked to a larger national identity, it was in keeping with the project's exploration of what "We the People" might mean to different minority groups as well as to a larger conversation about the role of minority ethnic communities in the new nation of Afghanistan.

To Azam, *Being We the People* was "just the name of the website, so the phrase or the title of the project in the beginning didn't mean a lot to me." But when pushed to consider what the idea meant to him, he said he saw it less as an assertion of Hazara pride or identity and more as a prompt to bring to light to the lives of everyday people, especially minorities, in Afghanistan: "It was a very good and comprehensive title, which we took to be what we wanted it to be . . . to introduce the people . . . [We] were not trying to extoll certain perspectives, we're not trying to make ways, or a campaign, or a mission; we were just trying to get [photographs of] these people, people who were living in Afghanistan, especially the minorities, and the minorities in the United States." Azam later said, "I think if we were told about it [the project] in detail at the beginning . . . we might have taken very different photographs." His recollection suggests that the Marefat students, perhaps because of the challenges of transnational communications and operations, did not receive or digest the emphasis on the minority imprint that the project designers originally intended.[67]

VISITING PHILADELPHIA: "A MID-PROJECT AUDIBLE"

Despite the different interpretations and impacts of the project and its guiding theme, the choice of photography as the central medium encouraged dialogue between the Kabul and the Philadelphia students.

Using the photography sharing website Shutterfly.com, they uploaded photographs that provoked discussions within schools and online. Samantha recalled, "Through photographs we really had the chance to see what life was like for them. We shared memories, experiences and most of all what made us all people."[68] A photograph of her sister, who has cerebral palsy, provoked an emotional discussion at Constitution High School as many of the students considered for the first time what it might mean to her life.[69] Samantha's photograph of her sister also led to a discussion of mental illness and disabilities in both countries. She asked her Marefat colleagues how these issues were understood and discussed in Afghanistan, and one student "estimated [that] 97 percent of Afghans had mental disabilities." Philadelphia participants were shocked. However, another Marefat student explained, "I think that more than twenty years of war has affected deeply on our people, and it has caused an increase of people who have mental disabilities. But now they are members of our society and people respect them as human . . . People who have mental disabilities need to be helped and have access as ordinary members of society, and here in Afghanistan we try to expand this culture of accepting all society members as equal." The discussion fostered an intimacy between the two project teams, which made the Marefat students' eventual trip to Philadelphia feel like the reunion of old friends.[70]

Originally, Allen, Stern, and other NCC staff had planned to travel to Afghanistan mid-project to spend time with the Kabul students. But after they recognized the depth of the discussions that were occurring via Shutterfly.com, they asked AAM and DOS to amend the original implementation agreement to allow ten Marefat students to travel to Philadelphia. Allen asked, "Rather than sending a bunch of American museum executives, myself included, our director of exhibits, and a couple of project consultants, to Afghanistan to provide technical museum assistance at the National Museum, wouldn't it be a much better thing if we actually got these students in a room together?"[71] The cost of insurance for staff traveling to Afghanistan, as well as security concerns about Taliban activity around the capital, also made going to Kabul both expensive and complicated. Even with this change in plans, logistics would remain complicated because the Marefat students did not have passports and it was difficult to obtain U.S. visas for Afghan nationals. Nonetheless, at the time it made practical sense to bring a group of Marefat students to Philadelphia rather than send Philadelphia staff to Kabul. The experience of Stern and Hormozi, when they traveled to Kabul toward the end of the grant to deliver the exhibit and help install it at NMA, confirmed these challenges.

According to Allen, an ideological consideration also factored into the decision to "call a mid-project audible." Stern explained, "I see a lot of this where people say, 'We're going to teach you how to do this.' And people saying, 'Well, thanks, but also I'm hungry; can you give me some food?' I think whatever capacity or lessons we could have taught them, they would have said, 'Great, thanks so much for coming, can you help us install a fire retardant system and a security system? And here are all the things that we need to protect our artifacts. Your lessons are great but . . .'"[72] In other words, NCC staff were making a conscious attempt to avoid replicating neocolonial power dynamics by unilaterally determining the course of the project. They also recognized that the school was operating in an entirely different public history context from the NMA, its partner museum, which had self-consciously identified its own significance and power. Still, the authority to make this change lay with the NCC, not with either of the Afghan institutions.

The "mid-project audible" that changed the planned activities had a significant impact on both the photography project and the people-to-people diplomacy relationships among students, teachers, and museum staff. Marefat students were able to engage in unscripted, face-to-face dialogue away from Kabul, with NCC staff acting as facilitators, and took part in an extended in-person workshop to pair the U.S. and Afghan photographs. Conversations were much deeper than the virtual dialogues had been. A planned half-day workshop extended into almost an entire day as the students discussed in English which photographs belonged together in the exhibition. They deliberated over what each photo meant for the students and their lives. In keeping with people-to-people diplomacy, the session focused predominantly on similarities rather than dissonance or disagreement. Cristella recalled fondly, "I don't know what I expected from that moment, but it ended up being half trip down memory lane, half storytelling hour, half—or I guess third,

third, third—opportunity to do the actual task of pairing."[73] Samantha corroborated this assessment: "The pairing of the photos was interesting because I didn't think we could pair them all. When we actually started to pair the photos everything came together. The similarities in each photo varied and that's what was cool about it . . . It allowed me to see our likeness in a different artistic way." These conversations and the goal of seeking similarities also produced another people-to-people diplomacy impact: it cemented burgeoning relationships. Reneé Jackson, a Constitution High School student, noted, "Coming into the project I expected to take photos, learn more of their country, . . . but I didn't think I'd be able to actually have a hands-on experience meeting them and understand how they are. That was really something and I made friends in the process."[74] Marefat student Fatema Jafari recalled that the project was transformative: "This project changed all of us." Royesh confirmed, "I think it was [an] eye-opening experience by all terms . . . They learned something firsthand about the kids in the U.S., about the dreams of their peers at a similar high school, they learned about their language, taste, and sense of understanding." Fekrat said that the trip helped the Marefat students "learn that ordinary people in the United States are like Afghanistan but very hardworking people, very punctual, very ambitious, and hopeful, and positive, and generous."[75] The results were so successful that both Stern and Allen later lamented that they had not thought of bringing the Marefat students to Philadelphia from the earliest planning stages.[76]

NOT FROM "WAR-TORN AFGHANISTAN"

The "mid-project audible" also gave the Marefat students another opportunity for identity negotiation and meaning making. It occurred at the studio of the NCC's media partner, local television station CBS-3, early during the students' visit to Philadelphia. In a closed discussion among the U.S. and Afghan students and the station's news anchor, Chris May, the Marefat students challenged May's headline from the previous evening's news: "students from war-torn Afghanistan." They "launched a veritable offensive against the CBS news team, who tried repeatedly, without any measure of success, to defend coverage of Afghanistan by the U.S. media in general and their network in particular." Recalling this event in the grant's final report, Stern and Allen concluded, "When the students' barrage of questions and smiling-incriminations would not cease, and only seemed to become more pointed, the news team realized that they were outmatched and, reluctantly, cried 'uncle.'" The report writers marveled at the moment when the CBS anchor "admitted, to the satisfaction of everyone in the conference room, that the American media's coverage of Afghanistan was, on the whole, sub-standard and devoid of nuance."[77]

Recalling these events five years later, Stern and Allen maintained their admiration for the students while celebrating that they had created an environment that had implicitly encouraged the students to speak out about issues that concerned them. Stern was impressed by the students' level of comfort, "To have been in this country for two days or a day or something, and to have the fortitude to rebuff a guy in a fancy three-piece suit at the head of a conference table, it was really remarkable. They didn't seem to be uncomfortable at all." The students demonstrated "a level of confidence to stand up for themselves, their ethnicity, and their country, that they [by Stern's assessment] did not have when the project began. The ten students showed, for the very first time, that they felt not only permitted, but *entitled* to have their voice heard." Allen agreed, also suggesting that this success was the result of not only NCC's embrace of the public historian as facilitator paradigm but also the choice of students as participants.[78]

Those moments in the CBS-3 studio were not the only examples of student-led dialogue. While visiting the Penn Women's Center, both groups of students engaged in discussions about differences in women's rights in the two countries. Recalling the threats made against her and other female students when they protested recent changes in Afghanistan's laws regarding women, Rabia, one of the Marefat students, broke down in tears. Allen recalled, "[Rabia's] response to [the other students' sympathy] was 'I'm not crying because I'm upset, I'm crying because this is the first time I could tell the story without fear or trepidation that something would happen to me for saying it.' And again this in front of some of the American girls and some of the American students, so it was all of these things coming together."[79] These moments revealed how successful the project directors had been at creating space for the participants to engage in self-driven dialogue and showed that the Marefat students were willing to wrestle with their identity as a persecuted minority who were also members of a larger nation.

In Philadelphia the Marefat students spoke of themselves as Afghans because few in the United States knew about the Hazara or the history of ethnic groups in Afghanistan. Royesh later suggested that this gave the students "optimism, courage, and self-confidence."[80] But speaking for both their country and their ethnic group also caused them some unresolved discomfort. Azam called it "a dilemma"; it was difficult to be addressed as an Afghan and to speak as a representative of a country that was "very difficult . . . to relate to the history of." He explained, "Inside Afghanistan I'm more attached to my ethnic identity, that's what's always been defining me in my role in society. So when I came to the U.S. this whole question of which one of these identities I would present more, was a question for me." He continued, "I tried so much not to look like I'm not representing the larger population, I'm representing Afghanistan, but I'm also representing a smaller minority, or an ethnic minority. For example, I tried my best not to think in a way that might somehow harm Hazara's image."[81]

EXHIBITING ETHNIC AND NATIONAL IDENTITY

The photography and travel experiences were not the only ways in which *Being We the People* led to identity formation and negotiation. The exhibition at the NMA provided a vehicle for this Hazara community to assert its own place in a large, new, national identity and to briefly insert itself into a national museum that had historically contributed to its silencing, even if this silencing had been more symbolic than real, given the few visitors to the institution. For the Marefat students, the NMA's symbolic role as a custodian of national history and an institution of the current government added even more importance. Although their photographs were not specifically of Hazara people or places and, in fact, documented many aspects of Kabul life, the opportunity to exhibit Hazara work in a museum that did not traditionally exhibit artifacts of Hazara history or provenance felt significant.[82] Azam said that the exhibition was "very important for me . . . It was an opportunity to show us as normal citizens, that we participate in these civil dialogues." The NCC staff and Royesh agreed, with Royesh also pointing out that the exhibition allowed the Hazara students, through their photographs, to "speak to" parts of Afghanistan society and an international audience to which they had previously not had access. "They could see their work on display for hundreds of important dignitaries, national and international."[83] Stern believed that the exhibition was one of the "most powerful things" about the project, especially in the aftermath of the Taliban's destruction of Hazara historic sites and the museum's archive of the nation's pre-Islamic history. The effect of the destruction had been felt throughout the Hazara community, underscoring the absence and active removal of the minority group's history from a larger national narrative.[84]

The initial grant proposal had included plans for sophisticated, interactive, "flex-ibit" technology that would allow the two concurrent displays to "talk to one another" and further the dialogue created during the development phase. While that was, in the end, not possible, the exhibition did maintain the guiding principal of multivocality.[85] In his short remarks at the NMA opening, Azam urged the visitors to explore the exhibition with the knowledge that the photographs would elicit different interpretations from different people: "I think the reason we did all of the photography is because we think each photograph has its own magic in it. And it speaks for itself, so I'm not here to tell you what we did or what we did not do, I'll let you watch the exhibition and see the photographs and get the message that they are trying to convey."[86]

Although the show's public reach was limited, most of those who did visit saw the photographs through the lens of Afghanistan's ethnic divisions. Massoudi recalled, "The significance of the project was involvement of students and presenting one of the communities from Afghanistan in the exhibition."[87] Royesh said, "There were people [at the opening] who would admire the works and the idea behind the exhibition. But there were also people that would show their surprise to see such a work from the kids of the Hazaras . . . You could see some audience [members'] astonishment for such an innovative project by the Hazara kids."[88]

The exhibition's impact on the public may have been limited by the NMA's broader lack of public engagement; but it was symbolically important for not only the Marefat students but also the NMA staff. Massoudi said, "[The museum] didn't have too many exhibitions at that time because it was in [the] process of reopening. Therefore, this exhibition was complementary of displays there. In addition, this exhibition was the first in [the] history of the museum that presented parts of culture from other countr[ies] and [the] work of students." He reflected that his favorite memory about the project "was the great opening organized together with Marefat High School. The students of this school were looking great when they were greeting guest[s] for the opening."[89] Hormozi and Stern also recalled the positive experience of assembling the exhibition with the Marefat students in the week before the opening and seeing the students win over the museum's small staff. Stern worried that underlying ethnic tensions might surface but was surprised by staff reactions. He cited an interaction between Massoudi and Royesh as an example of the goodwill established locally: "The director at the very end grabbed Aziz [Royesh] by the hand and wouldn't let him go, and said, 'This is the most well behaved group of people or group of students I've ever had here' or something like that. Everyone had tears in their eyes . . . and because I was so worried or maybe over-concerned about the ethnic tensions, [I] saw these moments as really powerful."[90]

The choice to present the photographs with limited captions to allow viewers to reach their own conclusions meant that the show was received very differently at the NCC from the way it was in Kabul. The exhibition was hung in Posterity Hall, between Signers' Hall and NCC's permanent exhibitions. Reviews suggested that most viewers were reading the photographs through a comparative "us versus them" national lens. Visitor reflections, as recalled by NCC staff and revealed in published accounts, elevated the Hazara to representatives of "war-torn Afghanistan," thus marginalizing their minority status. This mirrored the way in which the Constitution High School students' identities as minorities had been subsumed by their identities as U.S. citizens throughout project.

According to information online, "[v]isitors to the simultaneous exhibits were shown what being 'We the People' looks like to young minority citizens—in an established democracy, and in one emerging from decades of war," but the deliberate lack of interpretative text meant that similarities and differences between the United States and Afghanistan became the dominant interpretations. Perhaps reflecting her own intentions for the project, Cristella speculated that visitors latched on to the compositional and aesthetic similarities between the photographs: "I hear[d] them gushing about 'I can't believe how similar, I can't believe, some of them were so different. But the ones that were similar, those are the ones that really stuck with me.' Because it humanized people we only really hear about in the news for most people." She declared it to be the "best project I've ever worked on," and Allen, Stern, and Hormozi concurred.[91]

A June 2010 review also spoke of the photographs as representative of their respective countries, agreeing with NCC staff members' interpretation. The reviewer, Alex Irwin, described the exhibition as "an impressive but unassuming collection of 30 or so photo pairings," and "it really stands out for the quality of the photographs across the board—from composition to color to subject matter. This isn't the kind of exhibit where the work is impressive, 'especially for high school kids.' It's simply impressive—just be sure to read the captions, too." However, Irwin disagreed with Cristella's speculation that the show mostly drew viewers' attention to comparisons between the photographs. He instead argued, "It's the juxtaposition of these photos that really gives the exhibit its power. A photograph titled 'Tank Playground' of children climbing on armored vehicles half-submerged in sand on a beach outside of Kabul takes on a new meaning when paired with 'Day at the Beach'—a tranquil photo of an Ocean City, N.J. lifeguard boat in the surf."[92] Irwin's interpretation confirmed the Marefat students' and facilitators' hope that the exhibition would insert their voices into Afghanistan's civic discourse and represent their nation while also showing the rest of the world that living in Afghanistan involved more than just war.[93] But the review neglected to acknowledge that these photographs were taken by a minority group, an important element of the project for Marefat students. As one of them, Delaram, reflected, the exhibition had allowed her to engage not only in Afghanistan's civic discourse but in a larger global discussion: "Now I can announce my ideas to the people of the world by photography."[94]

Working with the NMA was notably significant for the Marefat students, but working with the NCC was not unusual for the Constitution High School students. While the Philadelphia students learned a great deal from the project, the existing relationship between the school and the museum and the complementarity nature of their missions meant that the exhibition and its location had less symbolic importance than it did for their colleagues in Kabul. Samantha recalled, "It was exciting to see our work displayed for people to see" but also that the opening of the exhibition "signified that the project was over, and that hurt a little, to be honest."[95] Despite such muted responses, the Constitution High School students believed that the project had had an impact on their lives and outlooks. Ian McShea, while misidentifying the location of Afghanistan, said, "I got to throw away all the stereotypes and all the feelings I had, especially about the Middle East. It's important for our generation to communicate on a global scale."[96]

EMBRACING PUBLIC CURATION

In the unlikeliest of transnational contexts, *Being We the People: Afghanistan, America & the Minority Imprint* provided a practical example of museums' embrace of "public curation."[97] Stern's pro-Hazara sensibilities, his support for Fekrat's idea for a photography exhibition, and his skepticism about international aid work in Afghanistan mingled with the NCC's model of dialogue, creating a desire among staff members to empower the Hazara students as agents of meaning making and content creation. The Marefat students, working within this framework, used the project as a means for negotiating their minority ethnic identities and claiming their national voices at home and abroad. This empowerment and negotiation became manifest thanks to the project's focus on dialogue, which the Marefat students took seriously during their trip to the United States. The pragmatic and ideological "mid-project audible" further highlighted the willingness of NCC staff to embrace change and let the project evolve. This allowed dialogue and shared inquiry to flourish in person as well as digitally. Yet the Marefat students' wrestling with and renegotiation of the project's themes vis-à-vis their own ethnic identity was not mirrored among the Philadelphia students. The ideologies of NCC staff members, their expectations for the project, and their sympathy for the Hazara effaced the Constitution High School students' minority status and framed them as representatives of the United States rather than as a specific minority community. These dynamics reinforced DOS's public diplomacy paradigm, which seeks to emphasize the nation-state imperative.

The Afghan public history context that has decentered museums as central to memory making as well as the NMA's beleaguered history and meager resources exacerbated the power dynamics embedded in the structure of Museums Connect. This meant that the NCC and its staff remained the major authority in administering the project and establishing the parameters of its components. The selection of Constitution High School and Marefat High School as community partners gave two groups of civically inclined students a similar education in civic engagement and learning through dialogue and ensured a relatively balanced relationship that allowed their work to become a shared inquiry. The NCC's willingness to create certain conditions for the Marefat students to engage in dialogue contrasted with its approach to its local students at Constitution High School. The choice of photography as the exhibition medium allowed the students' multiple perspectives to appear alongside those of their international counterparts and spark different interpretations. However, by elevating dialogue about the similarities and differences in the photographs and avoiding lengthy interpretive captions and exhibition text, the exhibition did not open viewers to a deeper exploration of the two communities' histories and the "minority imprint."

As in the other Museums Connect projects discussed in this book, people-to-people diplomacy goals loomed large over the project. Participants consistently celebrated the friendships and relationships that developed among students and staff members. At times the vigor and passion of these people-to-people connections seemed to overshadowed the exhibition and its development. For example, Stern and Hormozi later recalled that personal relationships were one of the most significant aspects of the project, and project facilitators from both countries suggested that it had had a long-term impact on themselves and the students. Allen said, "I think ultimately they [the students] are exactly what we aspire[d] for people—at the time—who came to the Constitution Center to be, which is active citizens. It's not our place to say how they are active citizens, but that they take an active role in the world around them, and we can see that in all of them." Royesh agreed: "The impacts of the project on the students, especially when they met each other face to face in Philadelphia, was beyond explanation. It was highly wonderful. The students would embrace each other with crying and tears in the eyes. That was the moment which none of the groups would forget."[98]

Eventually, the NCC exhibition was redesigned and installed at Philadelphia International Airport, where approximately 500,000 travelers passed by it. Yet in spite of both this visibility and the close personal relationships that developed during the project, the two museums have not maintained a long-term connection, and the institutional sustainability of the project remains unclear. Cristella lamented, "I wish it had [had] a more long-term consequence. They [NCC] had so much transition at the highest levels that the momentum didn't stay around the international work."[99] In 2011–12 NCC was invited to conduct another Museums Connect project and chose a partnership with the Natural History Museum of Latvia, which it based on its experiences with the NMA and Marefat High School. Since then, international programs at NCC have ceased to operate because of significant staff turnover.

CHAPTER 3

Beyond an "Imperialist Undertaking"?

Negotiating Transnational Public History Pedagogy

Sitting in the Ben M'sik Community Museum (BMCM) at the University Hassan II in Casablanca, Morocco, in December 2011, curator Julia Brock and I, both of Kennesaw State University's Museum of History and Holocaust Education (MHHE) in Kennesaw, Georgia, facilitated a discussion with university students affiliated with both museums about the stereotypes of Islam they wanted to address in the collaborative online exhibit *Identities: Understanding Islam in a Cross-Cultural Context*. All of the Moroccan students were Muslim, and most of the U.S. students were not. In a vibrant conversation the students discussed distorted images of Islam in the U.S. media, triggered by a small number of terrorists and religious fundamentalists; misunderstandings about the cultural and religious significance of the hijab; and confusion about the gender dynamics of contemporary Moroccan life. The Moroccan students' thoughts and ideas dominated this initial workshop, the first of a number that occurred throughout the week that MHHE staff and students spent in Morocco. Others sessions, also led and guided by MHHE staff, focused on exhibition development, including the creation of a concept statement, identifying the exhibition's "big idea," and best practices. These often-passionate conversations occurred nearly halfway through the second of two Museums Connect projects involving MHHE and BMCM between 2009 and 2012. Nonetheless, they epitomized the underlying dynamics at play in the partnership. Open and energetic dialogue played a significant role, but MHHE staff framed and facilitated the discussions, led instructional workshops, and guided the projects' progress, including the exhibition's development.[1]

Both of these Museums Connect projects practiced transnational public history education and allowed two very different university museums to build new audiences within their communities based on a shared exploration of Islam and Muslim identity. The projects were beneficial to faculty and students engaged in the development of practical public history skills and their implementation in high-stakes, real-world environments. The pedagogical activities—oral history, community program development, and online exhibit design—though rooted in U.S. academic public history practices, were altered and negotiated due to the confines of the grants' structures, the local contexts of both museums, and the need to conduct oral histories and exhibition development workshops for two very different institutions and their students.[2] The transnational partnerships did present power imbalances around professional training and assumed expertise, which emerged due to variations in museum culture and approaches to public history in the two countries, the choice of projects that placed public history pedagogy at the center, and the involvement of some MHHE staff in the creation of BMCM. Importantly, however, the partnerships also revealed a number of ways in which the Moroccan museum, its staff, and its students negotiated these power dynamics and brought specific skills to project activities to make them work within the cultural and museological contexts of Morocco in order to benefit BMCM and its community.

TWO MUSEUMS WITH CONNECTED HISTORIES

Situated in Ben M'sik, one of Casablanca's poorest neighborhoods, the BMCM, Morocco's first community museum, opened to the public in 2006. Its mission is "to preserve memory by interpreting, exhibiting, and promoting the stories and heritage of the diverse populations of its neighborhood and its region."[3] To connect the museum to the poor, mostly illiterate community, BMCM proposed to use its first Museums Connect grant to develop "creative, sustainable, and meaningful ways to engage the diverse working-class neighborhood in which it functions." The application noted that "[m]any Hassan II students live in Ben M'sik, but other community residents are largely excluded from the [walled] campus and, by extension, the museum."[4]

As I will discuss, a long history connects Moroccan museums to the west, but the BMCM and the MHHE also have a more personal connection. In 2005, University Hassan II administrators and members of its American studies department traveled to KSU to tour the MHHE. Catherine Lewis, MHHE's director, and Cindy Vengroff, its program coordinator, then visited Morocco to help guide university staff and local business leaders in planning their own museum. Lewis recalled, "When we got to Morocco it was clear that they wanted to build a museum, but they had no idea what a museum was, what it would look like, how it would unfold." So she ran a workshop on how to develop a mission statement and initiate plans, which she based on her own training in U.S. museum and public history best practices. The result was a proposal to develop BMCM's first exhibit, one modeled on MHHE's traveling exhibits. This inaugural show was collaboratively developed but designed and fabricated in the United States because, Lewis recalled, "a proficiency level in curation and fabrication techniques at Hassan II . . . [was] still emerging."[5]

The MHHE was created in the wake of the Holocaust memory studies boom of the 1970s. In 1993, after fifteen contentious years of discussions and debates around the United States, the U.S. Holocaust Memorial Museum opened in Washington, DC, and, in the words of the scholar Edward Linenthal, "the Holocaust became an event officially incorporated into American memory." At the same time, smaller Holocaust museums and education centers were opening across the country. In 1986 the Georgia Commission on the Holocaust was founded to promote "public understanding about the Holocaust"; and in 1996 the William Breman Jewish Heritage Museum opened in Atlanta, displaying its permanent exhibition, *The Absence of Humanity: The Holocaust Years, 1933–1945*. In 2003, the MHHE, originally called the Holocaust Education Program, was created at KSU in order to host the traveling exhibition *Anne Frank in the World* for the Georgia Commission on the Holocaust. That exhibition was on display for three years, 2003–6, in a purpose-built space within the university's continuing education building. Then, in January 2007, the MHHE unveiled a new permanent exhibition, *Parallel Journeys: World War II and the Holocaust through the Eyes of Teens*.[6]

Led by Lewis, a member of the history department, MHHE "expanded its mission [in 2007] to a more inclusive emphasis on promoting greater cultural awareness, tolerance and diversity." The museum aligned itself with the deeply contested definition of the Holocaust embraced by the U.S. Holocaust Memorial Museum, which had moved beyond a Jewish-only interpretation of the term that some of its advisory council members had advocated. Given that MHHE is a university museum, its staff have been driven by an impulse to educate rather simply memorialize. Its position within the university and Lewis's leadership mean that it also has consistently sought to use best practices developed within the ideological frames of U.S. museums and the North American academy.

KSU is Georgia's third-largest public university and is located in politically conservative Cobb County, only a few miles from the site of the nation's most famous anti-Semitic lynching: the 1915 murder of Leo Frank. In keeping with democratically derived ideas of civic society, MHHE maintains a central focus on reaching out beyond the university campus to engage different communities, including local residents and organizations. Since 2007, its mission has been

> [t]o present public events, exhibits and educational resources focused on World War II and the Holocaust in an effort to promote education and dialogue about the past and its significance today. Through educational dialogue about World War II and the Holocaust, our programs emphasize: multiple and complex human experiences; ethical and political consequences; respect for difference and diversity of life; and acceptance of civic and personal responsibility.[7]

In their first Museums Connect grant proposal, the U.S. applicants situated their proposed exploration of Muslim identity within this mission: "The fears and ignorance that generated the genocide of 70 years ago did not end with that war . . . [S]ince September 11, 2001, the Muslim community has become a target of hatred in the United States. The MHHE would like to do more to create the conditions that will prevent hate-filled actions and attitudes on our campus and in our community."[8]

The resulting project, *Creating Community Collaborations* (2009–10), was a comparative oral history collaboration between MHHE and BMCM, with museum staff and their respective students conducting interviews in their immediate communities to explore the experiences of Muslims. It was designed to promote "extended conversations" that would "change the perspectives of the participants, dispel stereotypes and correct misinformation, and remind us that trust comes slowly." Led by Lewis, the grant authors argued that the project would allow both museums to build a "foundation upon which additional activities will flow, notably 'Coffee and Conversation' programs to showcase what was learned from the oral histories." At the center of the proposal was the intention of both museums to engage in a process of shared inquiry: a collaborative, transnational, public history approach that would educate university students through the practical experience of learning about and conducting community oral history interviews.[9] Fulfilling their mandates as university museums, the institutions would train the students in oral history methodology via Skype, guide them in conducting interviews in their communities, and organize public programs to share their findings. Students from both museums would travel to one another's countries to engage in cultural exchanges and further develop their collaborative relationship.[10]

The museums benefited from a one-time surplus of funding at AAM to conduct a second Museums Connect project, *Identities: Understanding Islam in a Cross-Cultural Context* (2011–12), which built upon the work of the first one. Engaging students from both universities, it developed an online exhibition featuring the oral history interviews collected during the first project and photographs taken by students and curated in exhibition development workshops. According to the proposal, "student participants w[ould] master theory and practice of exhibition development" and "develop a broader knowledge of one another's cultures."[11] Like the first project, *Identities* featured a travel component that not only furthered cultural exchange but also included in-person exhibit development workshops to supplement those carried out via Skype.

SOMETHING MORE THAN A "STINKY CADAVER"?

Both the power relationships that emerged between the two museums and BMCM's modus operandi were heavily influenced by the historical context of Moroccan museums. These institutions followed a significantly different trajectory from the gradual and complicated movement of U.S. museums toward a civic, community-centered approach. Instead, both during and after colonialism, Moroccan institutions tended to exclude Moroccan and marginalized minority cultures' perspectives. A recent analysis of the journals of Moroccan diplomats traveling to Europe between 1786 and 1922 highlights the country's long and uneasy relationship with European museum practices.[12] The diplomats spent time in many major European capitals and their early museums, including the Royal Library and the Louvre in Paris, the excavations at Pompeii, and the Weaponry Museum in London; and their journals reveal a paradoxical mixture of reverence and criticism. The language of respect demonstrates a deep imaginative and intellectual connection between Morocco and Europe.[13] Yet according to the scholar Mohamed Jadour, the religious beliefs that formed the intellectual prism through which these men viewed the world ensured that they viewed Muslim and Moroccan customs as superior and regarded European practices of collection with contempt. For example, Ben Idriss Al-Amraoui, the envoy to Napoleon III, wrote in 1860,

> A man of reason would be surprised to know how much money they [Europeans] spend uselessly on looking for animals and plants, and looking after them, and on the maintenance of the places where they are put, especially when he realizes how miserly and thrifty they are. They wouldn't spend any money if they were not sure they would make some profit or contribute to the magnificence and power of their nation. But what use or magnificence is there in collecting dogs, pigs, monkeys, wolves and insects! And why preserve a stinky cadaver that has no use.[14]

Reflecting on Al-Amraoui's disdain for European collecting habits, Jadour concludes that the diplomats "did not want to recognize explicitly the pedagogical goals of museums and their role in disseminating knowledge, mainly because of their religious backgrounds and their traditional culture based on the belief that Muslims are superior to unbelievers."[15] Ironically, this contempt mirrored the orientalist, racialized exhibition of otherness or "other" that defined European intellectual representations of North Africa and the Middle East, including those developed in museums. The scholar Patrick Wolfe, commenting on this early period of European collection from colonies, writes, "If mapping fixed the world for European statesmen, museology brought it home to the European masses . . . [T]he two most important discourses in which nineteenth-century museums involved their publics were those of citizenship and empire. Moreover, the two were inseparable. Given evolutionary anthropology's all-encompassing phylogenetic hierarchy, any ethnological display was necessarily a statement about rank."[16]

In Morocco this uneasy relationship with western museums and collection practices was complicated by the implementation of French museological practices during the forty-four years (1912–56) of French colonial rule. Raymond Koechlin, the president of the Friends of the Louvre and an observer of Moroccan culture under the French Protectorate, wrote in 1917, "Let us not exaggerate, in truth Moroccan art is not dead, but it was sleeping. Without a doubt it was going to die when we intervened and taking it under our protection, we have awoken it." Koechlin's characterization of the French as saviors of a declining and supposedly homogeneous Moroccan culture ignored both local reactions and negotiations with French policies and behaviors, reflecting instead colonial power dynamics and discursive realities. According to Katarzyna Pieprzak, a scholar of Moroccan museology, "[a]t the discursive core of the museum project in Protectorate Morocco was a desire to create an institution that through collection and 're-education' would save slumbering local art from a certain death." These ideas underlay the foundation of Morocco's first museum, Dar Batha, created in Fez in 1915. Prosper Ricard, the head of the Protectorate Fine Art Administration, declared the museum's mission to be the collection of "the most interesting specimens of both urban and Bedouin artistic production that could serve as models for the work of restoration presently undertaken."[17] The arts and museum agenda of the Protectorate Fine Arts Administration was intricately tied to other elements of the larger French colonial endeavor. Pieprzak writes that creating *le Maroc utile* (a useful Morocco) "became a slogan in Protectorate Morocco that extended to all sectors of society, even to art. Indeed, the museum and its artisan ateliers worked to create both useful art and useful people." This movement reflected ideas of the role of the museum in nation making and reinforcing governmental power that was also driving museum cultures in the west.[18]

More than just a means of dictating taste and making Morocco useful to its colonial metropole, museums under the French Protectorate were useful tools for engaging tourists. Writing for the *Guide Bleu* in 1921, Ricard declared that the Fine Arts Administration had a "duty to help the tourist understand Morocco well." This argument also held sway in post-independence Morocco. As a result, according to Pieprzak and Samir El Azhar, museum administrators and the government have continued to neglect Moroccans.[19] Pieprzak argues that "museums created by the French Protectorate Fine Arts Administration as sites for the collection of authentic cultural prototypes turned into stagnant depositories and did nothing to reflect the post-independence energy and excitement to reassert and redefine what it meant to be Moroccan."[20]

After Morocco was established as an independent kingdom, some hoped that the thirteen stagnant national museums, which had played an important role in French colonial rule but had had little impact on the lives of ordinary Moroccans, could be redesigned.[21] Perhaps they could cast aside their role as repositories of antiquities and colonial intellectual power. But financial, personnel, and political barriers prevented such changes. The long legacy of European colonization in Moroccan museums and museum culture remains firmly entrenched and continues to influence those institutions in the twenty-first century. Most of them still exclude the public and remain distant from contemporary issues of Moroccan public life. Their predominant role is to serve international tourists.[22]

A 2004 survey revealed that 75 percent of Moroccans have never visited a museum.[23] El Azhar found this deplorable: "The Moroccan government needs to become aware of the important role such a museum could play, not only in the tourism industry, but also in making the Moroccan people proud of their history." Otherwise, he warned, they would continue to be "artificial institutions." El Azhar pointed out that "[v]ery few Moroccan museums meet even the most basic standards of museology common to North American, Scandinavian, European, or Asian institutions." Although he may have employed this rhetoric to differentiate and elevate the significance of the BMCM—a new approach in Morocco that Pieprzak terms "tactical museology" (practices that diverge from the nation's previous museological practices that can build civic space for citizens unaccustomed to engaging with museums)—it is nonetheless evident that the larger Moroccan milieu has historically not valued museums as educational institutions because of their legacy as tools of imperialism.[24]

There have been recent attempts to rectify these embedded practices. For instance, in 2011 King Mohammed VI created the National Museum Foundation, led by the prominent Moroccan artist Mehdi Qotbi, as an arm of the Moroccan Ministry of Culture. The foundation is responsible for the thirteen national museums in Morocco and has set out to make them a vital part of citizens' lives as well as a central part of the country's tourist industry. In 2013 Qotbi ambitiously declared, "We want these places to be accessible to all Moroccans, so they can take ownership of their culture." Although he made it clear that he recognized the challenges of changing a national culture and raising the necessary funds to achieve this goal, his appointment has excited many Moroccans who are thinking critically about the role of museums in society. Yet the challenge is enormous: in essence, he must combat the widely held perception that, in Pieprzak's words, "Moroccan museums are failed institutions."[25]

Morocco has approximately thirty museums, and not all mirror the trajectory of the thirteen national ones. A number of these smaller institutions have attempted to present historical narratives that rub against the official Arab-Muslim national one, which minimizes the importance of minority Christian and Jewish groups in Morocco's collective memory. For instance, the Belghazi Museum in Fes—"Ali Baba's Cave"—has worked to make itself more accessible to a wider Moroccan public, yet its pricing, methods of display, and reliance on traditional Moroccan class tropes continue to make this private space exclusive, albeit in a different way from the national museums. The Chaykh Omar Museum in Akka, the Museum of Moroccan Judaism in Casablanca, and the artifact collection at the Jewish Cemetery in Fes are victims of what the anthropologist Aomar Boum calls the "plastic eye" approach to viewing Moroccan history—that is, "things that might be important but should be ignored because of what trouble the observer can experience if he made notice of them." While these museums actively seek to present the discordant histories of Jewish Moroccans, they are largely ignored or ridiculed because they present narratives that run counter to the dominant government one. National memory in Morocco remains the domain of the Arab-Muslim majority, and access to those histories is still the purview of elites.[26]

TEACHING TRANSNATIONAL PUBLIC HISTORY

Both the MHHE and the BMCM wanted to reach out to their communities and engage them in conversations about issues related to Islam and what it means to be a Muslim in the U.S. south and in Morocco. Despite this shared goal, the partners had different audiences, and their work occurred within different museological contexts. The first Museums Connect grant, authored principally by Lewis, stated that the project would "educate individuals in Georgia about a culture and religion that is sometimes vilified by the local and community media." The need for this work was made apparent in public responses to the press release announcing the museum's receipt of the second grant. Larry Hogue, in a letter to the editor of the county's conservative-leaning newspaper, the *Marietta Daily Journal,* wrote disparagingly of Muslims: "It does not benefit anyone to attempt to make a poisonous snake your pet, to feed it, nurture it, and welcome it into your home. The hope that you can change its nature of biting and killing you is akin to ignorance of the laws of nature." Comments on the newspaper's web version of the press release reflected a similar hostility to Islam.[27]

Both grant applications emphasized the centrality of public history pedagogy and identified university students as the grants' primary audiences. Lewis, along with Jennifer Dickey (KSU's public history coordinator and an associate of professor of history) and Samir El Azhar (the director of the BMCM), selected teams of students from the American studies and English departments at the University Hassan II and from the history and American studies departments at KSU. Together, these teams would conduct a comparative oral history project and curate an online exhibition. During the first grant project, both groups of students were trained in oral history methodologies before conducting interviews with Muslim residents in their respective communities. During the second project, newly chosen groups at both universities were trained in digital exhibition methodologies and used the oral histories to form the basis of a digital exhibition.

The participating staff, faculty, and students shared reflections about the projects in publications, on the exhibition website, and in interviews with me, and their responses demonstrated a high level of personal and institutional satisfaction. The MHHE has a close relationship with KSU's undergraduate public history program; and Dickey, its coordinator, was on the project team for both grants, as was Lewis, who had previously directed the program and also holds a faculty position in the history department. Dickey noted that, unlike traditional internships offered to the university's public history students, the Museums Connect projects—especially the second one—gave participants "an opportunity to engage with students and faculty from our partner institution in an effort to reach out to new constituencies in both the United States and Morocco." In so doing, the grants gave students an unusual opportunity to learn a wide array of public history skills: "They read their assignments in advance, asked meaningful questions, and worked hard to become accomplished oral historians in a very short period of time." Dickey's positive reflection about the grants was undoubtedly linked to the fact that they provided thousands of dollars for her students to learn innovative public history practices, yet she also emphasized that "[a]lthough the acquisition of tangible skills was undoubtedly beneficial to the students, the opportunity to work with the faculty and students of the BMCM and their community in Morocco and in Washington, DC, was perhaps the most thrilling part of the project."[28]

Many of the students who participated in the projects cited working in a transnational environment as an interesting and powerful way to engage in public history, though all spoke of their experience in terms of museums and in the language of oral history and exhibition development. For instance, during the KSU students' 2011 visits to Moroccan museums, Robyn Gagne discovered that her U.S. public history sensibilities were only one way of interpreting the past. In her reflection she acknowledged differences in curatorial practice between the two countries but also unintentionally revealed an underlying western-centric view that sees Moroccan museum practices as deficient or substandard when compared to U.S. ones: "It was so interesting how museums are curated differently in Morocco . . . [T]here would be a case with some artifacts, a label written in French and Arabic with what the object was, and, if you were lucky, a date. There was very little interpretation."[29]

Dickey's recollections highlighted these intangible impacts on college students from different countries who were working together on public history projects, and they also suggested the potential of transnational work for developing global sensibilities and outlook. For KSU students this meant an increased critical awareness of the U.S. role in the world, more empathy for their Muslim counterparts, and more awareness of the pernicious stereotypes often associated with Islam: "[The students] developed an appreciation for the challenges and rewards of cross-cultural exchange as well as an enhanced awareness of the impact and perception of America, both good and bad, in the world." This evidence, and the observations recorded by the students in their journals and on the project blog, corroborated DOS's sponsorship of this program as a vehicle of public diplomacy. For example, KSU student Matt Scott, who had never left the United States before traveling to Morocco during the second grant, saw the experience as transformative, both in opening his eyes to a world beyond his own nation and in terms of how it informed his understanding of the collaborative project with BMCM. Traveling to Morocco, a predominantly Muslim country, completely transformed how he understood Islam at the time: "I was fortunate enough to be able to go to Morocco with the American travel team and that completely rocked my world in terms of how I even conceptualized the project that we were doing."[30]

During the Museums Connect projects, the Moroccan students and faculty traveled to the United States, and they developed skills as public historians during the oral history and exhibition development training sessions that both groups participated in via Skype. Chaimaa Zamat, a student who worked on the BMCM team, reflected, "I have . . . had the chance to get involved in many tasks, like doing transcription and translation of people's testimonies recorded by the previous team. These were the citizens' opinions about their daily life in the neighborhood, society, Morocco, and even the United States of America." Another Moroccan student, Soumaya Ezzahouani, said, "We have worked side by side to finalize the online exhibit's statement, to define the themes we have chosen and to select the exhibit's photos. I have learnt so many new things about museums and good online exhibits. The workshops were very fruitful."[31] The Moroccan students also changed their thinking about the potential role of museums in civic life. Meryem Bassi recalled, "Through the museum we kn[o]w how the previous generation lived. And through it the next generation will see us." Zamat poignantly considered the central role that museums might play in Moroccan communities: "I was impatient to see this new approach of museums, to understand how this project would develop the community in Ben M'sik, and to get involved in tasks related to the scholarship of museums. My expectations have come true because now I know that a museum is not only a place which displays artifacts to be shown to tourists and the elites but rather an open place for the public. It serves the community living in this neighborhood."[32]

FROM IMPERIALISTIC UNDERTAKING TO A SHARED INQUIRY?

In their proposals, the MHHE and BMCM grant applicants framed the projects as collaborative endeavors that would engage with recent literature in the fields of museum studies and public history that foregrounded a shared intellectual authority.[33] The goal was to collaborate on all of these explorations: between the museums, among the university students, and with the wider community. But there were challenges, given that the project's working language was English and that MHHE and KSU staff had greater expertise in conducting oral histories and using them in online exhibitions.

All of the Moroccan students and faculty who volunteered for the project were drawn from the English, history, and American studies departments, and they understood that their work on the project would be conducted in English. But their volunteerism reflected a significant personal commitment: Moroccan universities offer neither internships nor credit for extracurricular activities, whereas the KSU students received course or internship credit for their involvement. Although both museums were new to transnational collaborative projects, the

U.S.-trained public historians at MHHE did not share similar educational backgrounds with the faculty and staff at BMCM and the University Hassan II. El Azhar, BCMC's director, was a member of the university's American studies faculty but had received no formal public history or museological training before taking control of BMCM in 2006. In contrast, Dickey, Lewis, and Brock all had doctoral degrees and professional training in U.S. institutional public history practices. As principal authors and administrators of the grants, the KSU staff took charge of student instruction and led the day-to-day collaborative elements of the projects. This assumption of expertise and the elevation of U.S.-based oral history and exhibition development practices created distinct dynamics among the participants and shaped how the public history pedagogy elements were conducted.

Lewis recalled, "Samir [El Azhar] was deferential to us because of the power imbalance, because Samir had never done this . . . As we were writing the grant we were also giving Samir 'The Handbook for Small Museums.' It was professionalizing him [and] also the grant gave him credibility in a way that he did not have . . . before . . . The grant launched him into a much more national and international platform, and it became really important."[34] Dickey was also aware that a gap in public history education stood between the U.S. project facilitators and their Moroccan counterpart. She acknowledged that throughout the projects they tried hard "to help him [El Azhar] get up to speed in terms of being a museum professional."[35] Yet by attempting to correct the perceived power imbalance between the museums, MHHE staff further emphasized their positions as experts.[36]

In recalling the projects El Azhar also highlighted these different levels of professional training and suggested that the public history education that KSU faculty provided to the students was beneficial to him: "The project has marked a turning point in my professional life as coordinator of the Ben M'sik Community Museum. It has opened my eyes to the fact that museums should not be mere places where artifacts are displayed. They should be dynamic institutions that, on the one hand, maintain a dialogue with their local communities, and, on the other hand, establish international partnerships with museums around the world."[37] However, he pushed back against the KSU faculty's assumption of leadership in project activities. He later said that the BMCM's successful negotiation of both the local elements of the projects and the complex politics of the university and the community were as important as the collaborative work between the two groups of students.

These complex power relationships were clear to many people in Morocco, leading members of the faculty at University Hassan II to levy a charge of intellectual colonialism at the partnership program. As El Azhar explained, "[i]n the Arab and Muslim world, people are suspicious of programs sponsored or financed by the U.S. and Western countries." The faculty members called the suggestion to pay interviewees to elicit responses as "not academic" and "deontological." Yet, for El Azhar, the nature of the collaboration, the strong relationship between the two museums, and participants' willingness to adapt and negotiate the grant activities to fit their local contexts made the critique irrelevant: "Convinced of the objectives of the projects, we did not pay attention to criticism."[38]

Cultural differences and the projects' tight timelines meant that the lessons for students needed to be truncated, oriented toward practicality, and contextually adapted so that they were not solely a manifestation of U.S. intellectual colonialism. Lewis conducted oral history training for both groups of students via Skype: "We taught them the very basic issues of oral history. And we talked about some of the complicating factors of it. But we couldn't get too philosophical about it. We had to be just really, really practical: here is how you write questions, here's the technology, here's a consent form."[39] In other words, the process of teaching oral history did not simply reproduce the U.S. classroom context but was a new exploration in transnational public history that required both museums to adjust and adapt in order to produce new practices and outcomes.

BMCM students were preparing to interview residents of the poor, working-class neighborhood of Ben M'sik, a process that several recalled as an "adventure." Not only was BMCM a new museum that had only begun to establish itself in the area, but participants would be working in and exploring the authorship of a community that was not used to having its voice heard or contributing to the historical record. El Azhar said:

> People in Ben M'sik were not used to being interviewed. Working-class people and the rate of illiteracy is very high. People think that you are

> interested in them only in times of elections, and people come to see them only in times of elections. So they were suspicious and skeptical . . . the first time. And when we explained the aims and objectives of the program, and when we told them that we are interested in hearing [their] voice and hearing what do [they] think, and this is . . . an opportunity to tell their own stories, they said, "Why are our stories important?" Because they thought that it is only the powerful people, only the wealthy people, who can tell interesting things. But we told them that "we are interested in your stories because your stories are important to the history of Casablanca and we cannot understand Casablanca without your stories" . . . And they were enthusiastic about the idea. Someone whose voice has never been heard before, and you tell him that someone is interested in you and someone would like to know about your stories, not only in Morocco but elsewhere, so he becomes twice important: here and over there.[40]

In this way, despite the potential for rejection, participants were able to build support for BMCM within the community.

El Azhar and the BMCM students also needed to translate the proposed online exhibition activities into a version that was more suitable for their local context. Unlike the KSU team, El Azhar's was confronted by local citizens and the police, who were suspicious of the photographers and threatened them with arrest. The stark divide between the university and the community, made manifest by the campus walls as well as by different cultural views of photography, created serious risks for El Azhar and his students. Through negotiation and adaptation, however, participants were eventually able to instill "a feeling of pride" in the community. El Azhar noted, "[T]hey became aware of their importance as citizens who contributed to the economic growth of Casablanca and the independence of their country from the French."[41] Although this conclusion was anecdotal, it was supported by the way in which the public dialogue event showcasing the oral histories, "Conversations while Spinning Wool," captured the community's imagination. More than a thousand people attended the program.[42]

Development of the online exhibit rested on the work that MHHE staff conducted in workshops during travels to Morocco and the United States. The goal was to reflect the multivalent voices of the many participants involved in the project, both Muslim and not. *Identities* encouraged dialogue "[b]y exploring Moroccan and American identity through photographs, oral histories, conversation, and personal reflection" so that "we can learn about cultural commonalities and differences in a meaningful, open way."[43] It included many voices rather than an omniscient narrator. The photographic portion featured an equal number of U.S. and Moroccan photographs, grouped loosely into subthemes that spoke to facets of identity, which the museum teams had determined in conversation with one another. They were accompanied by Moroccan and U.S. oral histories placed side by side in a section titled "What We Learned." The exhibition gave equal space to the many different narrators interviewed during the first project, including Muslim residents of both metropolitan Atlanta and Ben M'sik, who reflected on their lives, the role of Islam in their homes and communities, and different portrayals of Islam around the world.[44] Minimal interpretation allowed visitors to wrestle with how to interpret these findings rather than depend on a dominant interpretive voice.

This approach did create some challenges. For instance, the imbalance in power between the two museums and their project teams became evident in March 2012, when they met in Washington, DC, for exhibit development meetings. Sitting around a conference table in the offices of AAM, six BMCM students and ten MHHE students debated the style, content, and symbolism of the exhibit's logo and graphic design. The logo would be the central graphic element representing the project, and all participants recognized its importance. Before this meeting, the MHHE project team had extensively researched designs and had chosen several prototypes, created by their museum's graphic designer. In those preparatory sessions, they had been drawn to abstract symbols, shapes, and colors that spoke to what they thought described the project and were also in keeping with best practices in website design.

But at the March meeting, one of the Moroccan students shared a different style of logo, one that included common Islamic symbols such as the crescent and moon, which explicitly referenced elements in the Moroccan flag. Dickey said, "Both teams brought design suggestions to the table, and it quickly became obvious that there was a wide gap between the two sides in terms of design aesthetics—shapes and colors had vastly different meanings for each team." Negotiations ensued: "We debated, for example, about whether or not to include representations of our national symbols (such as flags and colors) and of our faiths (such as the crescent and moon) and how best to express visually our values of collaboration and partnership." El Azhar said, "I think it was a cultural perspective. Each one believed in certain things or believed that certain things should be in the logo or shouldn't be in the logo. Some people believed a logo is a symbol but it shouldn't bear any cultural significance. But others—especially the Moroccan team—believed that it should highlight cultural aspects." He generously suggested that the teams got through this strained moment because of their close friendships and a spirit of cooperation: "[I]t wasn't a disagreement. It wasn't a conflict. It shows how honest the two teams were, and the matter was discussed in a very calm, serious, serene way."[45]

Julia Brock, however, believed that the tense interpretive debate over the logo highlighted an unease about underlying power dynamics: "Ultimately, though Moroccan students had created their own unique graphic pieces, it was the MHHE's designer who merged our ideas into one creation. This made some participants rightly uncomfortable—how much did the logo really reflect a compromise? Though all participants agreed on the final version, were our Moroccan partners eventually silenced because of our executive decision to pass the logo to the MHHE designer?"[46] The end product did feature some of the Moroccan students' color and shape suggestions, but its overall form was much closer to the MHHE team's original prototypes. The underlying power dynamics of the moment were certainly influenced by the relative professional capacities of the two museums and their staff members: MHHE has a full-time graphic designer, whereas BMCM has only one staff member. Moreover, the need to deliver a complete and punctual end product to the program's funders and administrators outweighed the desire for a more complicated process of negotiation and experimentation.

MISUSE OR STONE-SOUP DIPLOMACY?

Despite the power imbalances that played out during the grant projects, the Moroccan staff and participants were able to ensure that they reflected the BMCM's particular public history tradition and community relationships. For instance, the first grant set aside funds so that both museum teams could pay $50 to each oral history contributor. Although this is not a standard practice in U.S. oral history circles, Lewis requested these funds in the initial proposal, calling it "a small token but a token all the same."[47] The way in which this money was actually spent and how it was subsequently understood reflect the spontaneous yet culturally specific differences between the museum partners' environments.

For instance, rather than giving money directly to the contributors, as the signed documentation had specified, the BMCM team identified an acute local need and decided to spend the funds on computers for a neighborhood school. This move disturbed the MHHE team members, who knew that, despite the BMCM's best intentions, U.S. government money had been misused, which put the MHHE at risk as the grant's lead museum. Lewis saw it as "a big problem because it was not part of the grant." Dickey, too, was worried. She understood that the contractual acceptance of grant funding, especially from the federal government, does not allow for changes in how the money is spent during a project. After MHHE staff contacted AAM and sought clarification on how to handle the situation, however, they learned that there had been similar issues in other grant programs. Lewis later speculated that this one might have arisen for cultural reasons: Morocco values social history differently from how the United States does and possesses a different understanding of grant funding, especially when it comes from U.S. museums. She wondered if "[s]omehow paying the informants felt like an insult. It was shameful in some way. So it became a very contested thing."[48]

El Azhar did not share the MHHE team's anxiety about the legality of spending the grant money in ways not specified in the proposal or see it as improper or inappropriate. Rather, he explained that the challenge of conducting U.S.-style interviews among local residents was exacerbated by the need to follow Moroccan law, which prohibits public institutions from making cash gifts to the public. He did not learn about this law until after the interviews were conducted, when he had to tell the contributors that he could not give the money directly to them. After several meetings, the BMCM team and the contributors decided to use the funds to buy computers for a local elementary school. El Azhar said, "There was a feeling of pride in our team because we contributed to building something from which children of the Ben M'sik community would benefit. I believe this action is far better than giving a meager sum of money to some individuals who could have spent it on futile things."[49]

Mary Jeffers, a foreign service officer at the U.S. embassy in Morocco at this time, later said that the BMCM's actions were in keeping with DOS's hopes for cultural diplomacy programs such as Museums Connect. The situation reminded her of the European folktale "Stone Soup," a fable about the power of the collective after an initial investment piques curiosity and inspires action: "[BMCM's decision-making] was so impressive. So it was an outgrowth of the museum project, . . . because of the stipend, . . . [which] was almost like the stone of the stone soup, but it was also an outgrowth of this kind of self-empowering feeling that I think that the museum project helped to encourage. I don't want to say that it, the museum project, generated the entire community sense of wanting to do something in the community. But I think that it played a role."[50]

In the same vein, the BMCM team decided to change the name of the proposed "Coffee and Conversations" event that would present the oral histories recorded in Casablanca. El Azhar explained that calling the event "Conversations while Spinning Wool" tapped directly into Moroccan culture and would allow the museum to connect more effectively with its community: "This title has strong cultural connotations as it is borrowed from the oral tradition and heritage of the Moroccan people . . . This proverb is used whenever a person indulges in a task and he/she speaks at the same time. In the past, women used to meet to spin threads of wool. While spinning, they discussed various topics related to their everyday life. Therefore, this social gathering enabled them to help each other, exchange information, and discuss social issues." In his view, the name change did not affect the underlying intention of the program as it was laid out in the grant: "[E]ach team has chosen a title that springs from its social and cultural context, yet both teams strive to achieve the same objective: that is, to establish strong bonds of friendship and communication between their respective museums and communities. Despite the constraints of the contract, we were able to adjust some terms to our own cultural context." The new title did, in fact, appeal to residents of the community; nearly a thousand people attended the event, including local political officials as well as "students and their families, interviewees and their families, interviewers and their families, professors from the different departments, university administration staff, and people from the Ben M'sik neighborhood." "Conversations while Spinning Wool" gave the BMCM the opportunity to enact its mission as a community museum, to "function as a locomotive for the neighborhood by . . . [helping] its inhabitants to develop an awareness of themselves as actors and participants in the development of our country as a whole." El Azhar later said that the success of the grant projects also helped to convince skeptical colleagues at the university that the museum should be actively engaged in the community rather than a static repository of artifacts.[51]

"BROTHERS AND SISTERS"

In addition to the pedagogical benefits of these two grants, Museums Connect's people-to-people public diplomacy had an important impact on the participants. Dara Vekasy, a KSU student who participated in the second grant project, noted, "This . . . has been so integral to exposing me to different ideas and cultures than I have ever been able to experience before." Several Moroccan students said that their involvement in the projects continued to shape how they thought of themselves and their Muslim identity. Ismail Chaki reflected, "I can say for myself that the project had an impact on me. Firstly, working on a professional project such as that, which was my first experience of such a kind gave me a certain maturity in the way I handled my life."[52] Waafa Akir said that the program had made a profound difference in how she viewed herself vis-à-vis the U.S. students: "Yes, we are different, yet we can love each other, we can live with each other. After all we are all Allah's children. Before this trip I considered everything to be either black or white. If we don't think alike, we don't worship the same God, we don't share the same values or principles, we will not be able to understand each other! That was silly!"[53]

The Moroccan and U.S. students forged deep friendships, another benefit of working on a transnational public history project with a public diplomacy agenda. Robyn Gagne later said that working side by side with the Moroccan students during the travel portions of the *Identities* grant helped them build strong relationships: "We all felt like we had made good friends, and it was hard to part, but we all exchanged Facebook information and have kept in contact since we parted ways. As I hugged Zineb, I told her that this was not goodbye but we would see each other again. Zineb and I cried together." In these ways the grants effectively served their primary audience—university students—and "prepare[d] project members on both sides of the Atlantic to educate others about cross-cultural and community-based museum partnerships."[54]

This conclusion was confirmed by the facilitators, who praised the projects' success at creating deep personal bonds. Recalling the Moroccan team's trip to Washington, DC, Lewis said, "I don't think the website for the second grant is the thing to celebrate. I think it was the process, . . . seeing these working meetings, maneuvering through them, eating together, taking them around, traveling, . . . that we would get out in the evenings and go to dinner, and people would still be talking about the website and the logo and what they had in mind. It just resonated more."[55] El Azhar echoed these glowing reflections: "With the travel component it was of paramount [importance] because not only do you see the person, you shake hands with him, you hug him, you talk to him, you spend days with him, and you share moments with him. And it was very important for the students."[56]

Despite a historically friendly relationship between the United States and Morocco, there was a rise in the number of Moroccan-linked terrorist attacks, which have gained significant visibility in the U.S. media after 9/11. In May 2003 attacks in Casablanca killed thirty-three people, and Moroccan citizens were connected to the March 2004 terrorist bombings in Madrid. In a 2004 *New York Times* article, the journalist Elaine Sciolino noted that many European countries are now paying close attention to Moroccan affairs: "Moroccan groups have been seen as central to the terrorist threat in Europe, forcing intelligence and law-enforcement officials to adjust their strategies." In approving the partnership between MHHE and BMCM, DOS cited Morocco's proximity to the Middle East, and worries about young Moroccans joining Al-Qaeda as reasons to fund the projects. According to Mary Jeffers, "amongst ordinary Moroccans there's anger at the United States about our policies in the region."[57] Thus, it has been important to encourage the kinds of people-to-people interactions that took place in these Museums Connect projects.

The people-to-people relationships developed during the projects extended to the facilitators. In separate conversations Lewis and El Azhar both used the same metaphor to describe the bonds of friendship that had developed between them as a result of three years of collaborative work. El Azhar said, "Human relationships are important, they stay. We are more than friends, I always tell our colleagues in Morocco and America, with Dr. Jennifer [Dickey] and Dr. Catherine Lewis we have started as colleagues, then we became partners, and now we are brothers and sisters . . . We still exchange e-mails on family matters and we are ready to start another program if we have the opportunity to do that." Lewis likewise recalled, "Frankly, the absolute highlight was walking with Samir where he said to me—I think we were in D.C.—and he said, 'Catherine, we started as colleagues, then we became friends, and now you are my sister.' . . . And that told me we had done something right."[58]

FEELING FORSAKEN: QUESTIONS OF SUSTAINABILITY

Despite the success and depth of the friendships forged during the projects, sustaining that momentum proved to be challenging.[59] During the three-year period in which the projects were conducted, students were moving through their undergraduate programs and the public history certificate program at KSU, which meant that different students worked on each project. Pedagogically, this turnover created challenges in the development of the online exhibition. Lewis explained the facilitators' reasoning when they applied for their second grant: "We thought 'what if we use the oral histories'—we don't discard them—but we use them as the basis for an online exhibit, and really dig a little bit deeper into these questions of identity: What's really shaping the way these students feel about who they are in the world? In their community? In their family? And in this global community? So it was a great idea, but I think one of the big challenges with it was that we didn't have the same students." In other words, "[o]ur hope for depth was trumped by the reality of 'We've got to start over.'"[60]

The one-year cycle of Museums Connect projects and the clause that prohibited museums from applying for additional grants until three years had passed presented significant financial challenges for the MHHE-BMCM projects. Their ambitious scope and the cost of working across international boundaries—especially traveling with large groups of staff and students—made them difficult to replicate and sustain. Dickey acknowledged, "We haven't really done anything with the museums since the project ended because we haven't had the money to really do much . . . We will continue to work together and continue to be friendly with him [El Azhar], but we will not be able to travel back and forth without grant money."[61]

El Azhar agreed that a lack of funds has made further large-scale collaborations unviable. Yet "[t]o tell you the truth, I sometimes feel that I have been forsaken by my friends and partners . . . Some projects do not necessarily require money as the [Museums Connect] projects [did]. To illustrate the point, we had worked before with the[m] on a traveling exhibit. The whole work was done online. We can find other sources to finance these small projects." He continued, "I believe that there are a number of projects, although small, that we can set up."[62] He was correct; eventually the two museums did find a way to conduct two smaller projects: a traveling exhibit about Morocco in World War II and an online exhibit focusing on the transatlantic slave trade.

Team members discovered that the community engagement requirement of Museums Connect grants could be difficult to sustain once the grant money had run out. BMCM was founded specifically as a community institution and has continued to work directly with local residents, but MHHE has struggled to maintain its outreach in the Muslim community. After the *Identities* project was completed, the museum spent the next eighteen months participating in two different projects with the Muslim community in Georgia. In a KSU undergraduate oral history class project taught by Brock, students interviewed members of a local mosque, and MHHE won an American Library Association "Muslim Journeys" bookshelf grant, which brought a cohort of twenty-five adults from the community together over a three-month period to participate in a book-club roundtable. Although these efforts allowed the museum to continue exploring contemporary issues surrounding Islam in the region, Brock acknowledged that those involved were limited in their ability to link the larger community to the museum and were also suffering from a lack of larger institutional support. Additionally, without the Museums Connect grant money, MHHE could dedicate fewer staff to projects beyond its core mission of interpreting World War II and the Holocaust and thus has placed less focus on its broader mission of celebrating diversity and tolerance. During interviews museum staff acknowledged and lamented these challenges, reflecting that it has been difficult to maintain energy, momentum, and community connections when resources are removed. Dickey said, "If you were to go out and talk to people in the Atlanta Muslim community, most of them still aren't going to know who we are, they're not coming out here to see our programs or our exhibits. We don't factor into the conversation. We're just not a player in that world in the broader scheme."[63]

ROSE-TINTED GLASSES?

In a 2012 book published in Morocco to accompany the *Identities* project, I optimistically declared that the student participants "not only developed the curatorial skills necessary to create an online exhibit, but they also developed a deeper understanding of Islam and what it means to be a Muslim both in the American South, and also in Morocco."[64] Certainly, I was wearing rose-tinted glasses: I had been involved with two grants that had given the MHHE and the BMCM nearly $150,000 to construct innovative and exciting partnerships, extend their pedagogical offerings, and enhance careers, including my own. Nonetheless, the reflections of the other team members support my conviction that this was a rich way of learning and enacting public history pedagogy. The international partnerships allowed students to develop their skills and expand their global consciousness. The students' reflections emphasize the role that these projects played in encouraging greater cultural awareness and a better understanding of how working in different communities can affect public history projects. Furthermore, they show that strong friendships and productive collegial relationships developed among the two museums' students, staff, and faculty.

The MHHE took the lead in directing project activities because its staff members recognized that they possessed more professional training and operated within a broader museological context. These conditions, as well as staff members' contribution to the creation of the BMCM, structured the nature of the public history pedagogy. Such uneven distributions of institutional power were embedded within the Museums Connect program, given that it was funded by the U.S. government and administered by AAM. However, the partnership between the MHHE and the BMCM also revealed that it is misguided to assume that U.S. ideas and actions are passively absorbed abroad. Regardless of the power differentials and the different museological traditions, the BMCM successfully negotiated its activities within a local cultural context. The pedagogical activities, though deeply rooted in U.S. public history practices, were subject to alteration and negotiation due to the confines of the grants' structures, the local contexts of both museums, and the act of having to conduct oral histories and exhibition development workshops for two very different museums and their students.

Varying reactions to the use of oral history money in Casablanca highlight the difference in cultural and societal norms surrounding public history in the two countries and elucidate the different intellectual worlds occupied by the two museums. Likewise, the challenges of sustainability that both museums' staff acknowledged but interpreted differently bring into question the long-term impact of these grants. While all involved claimed that the projects were a great success, both museologically and diplomatically, their long-term sustainability, a stated goal of AAM, is much less clear.

CHAPTER 4

Activating Sites of Conscience

Addressing Shared Silences within Parallel Public Histories

In 2010–11 the Birmingham Civil Rights Institute (BCRI) in Birmingham, Alabama, and the Nelson Mandela House Museum and the Apartheid Museum in Johannesburg, South Africa, received a Museums Connect grant for "The International Legacy Youth Leadership Project." Students and museum staff from both communities traveled to each other's countries to undertake a shared exploration of the nations' histories, similarities, and differences, which included visits to historic sites of conscience.[1] Unlike the projects between museums in the Philadelphia and Kabul and Kennesaw and Casablanca, this one involved museums and communities that had similar public history practices and a shared language. The centrality of English in South Africa, while a problematic legacy of European colonization, was in this case an aid in reducing the power dynamics that had favored the U.S. museums and their communities in the other projects. Along with the historic connections already in place between Birmingham and Johannesburg, this created a more equitable relationship.

During the Alabama team's trip to Johannesburg, both groups of students visited the Apartheid Museum to explore the galleries and learn more about South Africa's apartheid past. Reflecting on this powerful emotional experience, Ahmad Ward, a project facilitator and the head of education and exhibitions at BCRI, admitted to having to "deal with a little bit of anger." He recalled: "I thought I had a fair knowledge of the apartheid situation, but it was an eye opener. This is absolutely ridiculous that this is one of things that happened in that country . . . I think everyone should go and see it." Ward's experience emphasized the emotional impact of learning about the racist past of a country other than his own. For the U.S. project facilitators, it also revealed a larger sensibility, one that permeated the grant and shaped its power dynamics. As Ward's comment demonstrated, he was not acting as an omniscient authority on the histories of the two countries. "It was a very enriching experience for me as well as the kids. At the end I got as much out of it as they did."[2]

The reflection-in-action of BCRI staff was only one facet of the complex web of power relations that existed between the museums and students during the project. Given the communities' similar public histories, the dynamic between the partners was relatively equitable—though there were notable discrepancies in how the institutions addressed youth programming. Their similar interpretive approaches allowed students to engage in a shared exploration of the civil rights and anti-apartheid movements that extended beyond popular interpretations of the movements' "great men" (Nelson Mandela and Martin Luther King, Jr.) to directly consider issues of race during these eras. However, these complex historical explorations did not translate into larger project outcomes. The grant's abbreviated time frame, coupled with its focus on the two communities' histories, prevented students from engaging in any significant discussion of contemporary issues of race. Such wider discussions were mostly absent from my interviews with participants and facilitators, nor did they take place during the teams' visits to sites of conscience. This was particularly apparent during BCRI's Nelson Mandela Day celebration, the grant's capstone event. During this program, which was open to the public, the students shifted away from complex layers of exploration toward a focus on Mandela. While his popularity as an international figure of peace gave the museum a way to engage with new communities in the city, the celebration's preoccupation with him as a figure effaced a deeper understanding of the two movements and their parallels.[3] In other words, although the Mandela Day celebration as well as spontaneous encounters between Apartheid Museum staff and the Birmingham public were effective at reaching out to local communities, the encounters may or may not have had a long-term impact on such relations. Nonetheless, they revealed that another project between museums and communities with shared histories and historic connections could have the potential to forge deeper community bonds.

"WE HAD A GLITCH!"

The Museums Connect grant gave BCRI the opportunity to emphasize the international part of its mission and expand upon its preexisting "Legacy Youth Leadership" program. Priscilla Hancock Cooper, at that time the museum's vice president of institutional programs, explained, "Our mission is to promote civil and human rights worldwide through education. This was a unique opportunity for us to bring our mission to life. We have a strong commitment to young people. And we have been looking for ways to activate—programmatically—that portion of our mission. It's a fabulous mission, but how do you do that? This was a wonderful opportunity to make real connections." Yet there were problems from the beginning. AAM had emphasized that the project should be reciprocal in nature, not a version of U.S. cultural imperialism, but the staff at the Mandela House Museum were inclined to be deferential. BCRI's project director, Laura Anderson, paraphrased a typical interaction with the director, Ishmael Mbhokodo: "Anything y'all want to do will be fine. It would be beautiful. It would be wonderful. Just tell me what you want to do and we're going to do it."[4]

Both countries had an established tradition of oral history, and the South Africans' experience with the Truth and Reconciliation Commissions—a central focus of the proposal—meant that they were familiar with developing oral history projects. Nevertheless, the partners struggled with problems of reciprocity and equality during the design stage.[5] The BCRI already had a vibrant youth program upon which to build (the "Legacy Youth Leadership" program); the Mandela House Museum did not. Instead, Mbhokodo told Anderson that he would find children from the museum's mostly black Soweto neighborhood to participate in the project. This created a power imbalance from the outset, as the BCRI staff clearly had more expertise in youth programming and in conducting a project of this scale. Anderson recalled, "[W]e already had this vibrant youth program in place here, and graduates of it, alumni of it, [and] we're going gangbusters over here. And all we're going to do is add this wonderful new dimension to it, and he doesn't have a youth program. But he thinks it's the greatest idea ever. He's totally on board. But then we're feeling guilty because it's not reciprocal."[6]

Concerns about capacity and qualifications became more acute when Mbhokodo, who had co-authored the grant proposal with BCRI staff, left the Mandela House Museum before the $120,000 grant was awarded in the summer of 2010. This period of confusion and anxiety threatened the project before it began. Anderson said, "I sent Mr. Mbhokodo a 'yippee!' kind of an e-mail and [got] no response." Cooper ruefully recalled, "We had a glitch! . . . For several months after receiving its MCCA award, the . . . project was on hold due to changes in governance at the original non-U.S. partner institution, the Mandela House Museum."[7]

There were other complications too. Originally, the Mandela House Museum had been managed by the Soweto Heritage Trust, founded in 1997 to "establish a cultural precinct in and around Orlando West, Soweto, and an overall promotion of Soweto and Johannesburg, in the contest of identity, pride, public awareness, the encouragement of tourism and economic upliftment." But in 2010 the government gave temporary custody of the house to the Apartheid Museum, which had opened in 2001 with the mission of "illustrat[ing] the rise and fall of apartheid." This change led to a labor dispute that created challenges for BCRI staff as they tried to move ahead with the grant's implementation agreement and start project activities. In an attempt to figure out the situation, Anderson and several BCRI colleagues decided to travel to Johannesburg to meet with the Apartheid Museum's deputy director, Ruwayda (Wayde) Davy, in October 2010, two months after the grant was supposed to have begun. BCRI staff wanted to learn about the changing administration of the Mandela House Museum and consider the feasibility of developing a project in an entirely different institutional and political context. As it turned out, this trip was instrumental in allowing the Museums Connect project to happen.[8]

The four-person BCRI delegation included Anderson and Cooper as well as Angela Craig, the coordinator of youth programs, and Lawrence Pijeaux, then the institution's president and chief executive officer. They met the Apartheid Museum staff, and spent considerable time with Davy, who oversaw the museum's educational programs. The BCRI team began to realize that their museum had greater similarities with the Apartheid Museum than it did with the Mandela House Museum and that this new partnership would be a better fit for the Museums Connect project. Like many house museums devoted to important national figures, the Mandela House Museum is essentially a shrine to a single central person.[9] In contrast, the Apartheid Museum, like BCRI, focuses on a broader interpretation of apartheid and the anti-apartheid movement. According to its website, "[a] series of 22 individual exhibition areas takes the visitor through a dramatic emotional journal that tells a story of a state-sanctioned system based on racial discrimination and the struggle of the majority to overthrow this tyranny." In contrast, the Mandela House Museum's mission is "to provide an effective, efficient and meaningful experience to all visitors, informing them of President Nelson Mandela's story, both in the context of his home, and in the context of his life as a whole, in a manner that promotes human rights, democracy, reconciliation, mutual respect and tolerance amongst the peoples of South Africa." BCRI, for its part, has moved beyond focusing on the great men of the civil rights movement to "enlighten[ing] each generation about civil and human rights by exploring our common past and working together in the present to build a better future."[10]

In terms of physical size, staff size, and reliance on grant money for programming, the Apartheid Museum and BCRI were very similar. As Anderson said, "we just had a lot in common." Yet she recognized the precarious nature of the partnership and the possibility for failure: "Given that the Apartheid Museum had no youth programs in place, the commitment was tremendous, for staff would essentially build the South African side of the project from the ground up." Davy also recognized this possibility: "We had taken over management of Mandela House Museum and this project was on the table already. It initially was a project between Mandela House Museum and the Birmingham Civil

Rights Institute. So in effect, we had inherited the project and therefore included the Apartheid Museum as a partner."[11]

The BCRI emphasized their desire to work with the Soweto neighborhood and build upon the historic connections between its youth and the youth of Birmingham. Anderson said, "[T]he whole concept of the proposal was based around the . . . idea of Birmingham-Soweto and their common histories, common experiences, and their [individual] histories." Thus, although the Apartheid Museum and its staff became BCRI's central partner, Soweto youth and the Mandela House Museum remained important to the project. Davy's colleague at the Apartheid Museum, the archivist Jacqui Masiza, was excited to be involved: "I . . . love working with the youth, and this was an opportunity to do exactly that. As the project was initially from Soweto and a first for our Museum, we had to make a selection from schools around the area, and I am quite familiar with the areas as I grew up there."[12]

SHARED PUBLIC HISTORIES

After the BCRI delegation returned to Birmingham, the Apartheid Museum staff announced that they were willing to go ahead with the project. Thus, the "International Legacy Youth Leadership Project" began work in 2011 with the stated goal of "engag[ing] the youth, museum staff, veterans of both movements, educators, community leaders, and the local community in a series of activities designed to increase knowledge and understanding of the parallels between the Civil Rights Movement in Birmingham and the anti-apartheid struggle in Soweto, the dynamic role of museums in interpreting those struggles, and the implications for citizens today."[13] As the language of the grant made clear, the shared histories and public histories of the two communities were central to how the grant was conceived and how the participating museums understood their relationships to one another.

Racial apartheid in the United States and South Africa spanned different historical eras but were similar in their impact on their nations and on individuals. More recently, they have also shared similarities in how they are interpreted at public history sites.[14] During South Africa's apartheid rule (1948–94), museums contributed to the systematic oppression of black and "coloured" South Africans through the implicit demonstration of power inherent in the creation and elevation of white supremacist historical narratives and the silencing of non-white histories. They were not the only public history sites to reinforce the government's racial binary. Monuments such as the Vortrekker Monument in Pretoria, which has been a site of contestation since 1994, were constructed as part of "an urban landscape of power" to reinforce white supremacy.[15] The Vortrekker Monument contributed to the heroic Boer origin myth of the apartheid state and depicted black Africans as savages needing to be civilized by the Dutch-based vortrekkers. The prominence and preponderance of these sites stood in contrast with the few public history sites that presented dissonant narratives.[16]

After the apartheid regime fell and the nation held its first democratic elections in April 1994, dominant dynamics of oppression and historical silences were challenged. Nonwhite South Africans, demographically dominant, became central actors in reshaping the nation's historical narratives and the way in which public history sites interpreted the nation's past. Yet as the public historians Andrew Hall and Cynthia Kros warned in 1996, to see the overthrow of apartheid as the end of oppression was to ignore the "quieter" legacy of white supremacy. In the last years of the apartheid regime, museum administrations were divided along the tricameral system adopted in 1986 by the Botha government, which gave limited power to the Indian and "coloured" populations, along with the white population, but not to the black population. These political and institutional entanglements continued to exist as the nation transitioned to democracy. According to Hall and Kros, "whilst the multiplicity of administrative divisions within the realm of cultural administration in South Africa may not seem alarming to outsiders, it must be remembered that they are based on racial rather than geographical divisions and that several administrations, most of them representing narrow racially based interests, can and do operate within the same geographical area." Only slowly did museums, historic sites, and monuments come to play a significant role in the transition to a democratic government, helping the wider population deal with the traumatic past and redefine the meaning of the new post-apartheid state. As Annie Coombes writes in her seminal account of public history during this era, these new public histories "effectively inform[ed] changing definitions of 'community' and 'nation.'"[17]

Within this transitory atmosphere, a "new exhibitionary landscape" emerged at important museums like the District Six Museum (founded in 1992), Robben Island (founded in 1997), and the Apartheid Museum (founded in 2001). Here, the racially inclusive nation sought to process and interpret the traumatic past that for many South Africans included "the experience of detention, displacement, or unannounced police harassment in the dead of night." This new approach has its critics. For instance, Crain Soudien argues that the nation's new history, by attempting to produce "triumphant and redemptive" revisionist narratives, continually reproduces the apartheid era's "artificial construction of apparently homogeneous ethnic constituencies," with the effect of diminishing "other forms of viable community."[18] The interpretation of apartheid, as told through its museums, monuments, and historic sites, was also contested before and after the democratic elections that swept Mandela and the African National Congress (ANC) into power and pushed the apartheid-enforcing National Party to the margins of South African political life. Fervent debates were conducted in the national and international media, and monuments such as the large bust of National Party president J. G. Strijdom in Pretoria became symbolic sites for protest and counter-protest, with one side trying to destroy them and the other trying to protect them.[19]

Contestations over the meaning of apartheid also materialized during the creation of new interpretive sites to commemorate the physical landscape of the apartheid regime's imprisonment, displacement, and abuse. Robben Island had been a prison in which many ANC members, including Mandela, had been confined; and turning it into a museum was contentious, given the numerous stakeholders with a share in its production of a national history as well as the tension between public and private enterprise on the island. Well-publicized clashes ensued among how to privilege ex-prisoners' memories, the desire of private businesses to turn the prison into an economically viable tourist attraction, and the new government's objective to commemorate the island as a symbol of national regeneration.[20]

Another significant public history site, the District Six Museum, did not easily fit into the new South Africa. District Six had been a culturally vibrant, cosmopolitan, economically diverse, and mostly "coloured" neighborhood in Cape Town that became a defining symbol of apartheid when the regime's Group Areas Act forced its residents to leave. Between 1968 and 1982, most of the homes in the district were leveled. Given this historical background, the District Six Museum—a founding member of the International Coalition of Sites of Conscience—was reluctant to follow the nation's traditional mode of public history presentation. Instead, it has become "a significant venue for community regeneration" through a bottom-up challenge to traditional hegemonic and hierarchical narratives. Using oral histories and engaging community members and visitors to share their experiences of the neighborhood, the museum has sought to heal and regenerate a community that was decimated when the area was racially zoned, causing "more than sixty thousand people to be forcibly removed from their homes."[21] The museum has asserted a land claim under the Restitution of Land Rights Act and challenged traditional national histories and narratives. The South African public historian Ciraj Rassool contends that this independent status has "enhanced the possibilities of constituting a vibrant, independent, contested public culture." Indeed, the museum has come to play an important role in post-apartheid public history as "an independent site of engagement, a space of questioning and interrogation of the terms of the post-apartheid present, and the institutions, relations, and discourses embedded in its production and reproduction." Independence from traditional hierarchies of knowledge and power is essential for the District Six Museum as it seeks to represent silenced communities that were historically omitted from these institutions.[22]

Such negotiations have also occurred at the policy level, as exemplified in the bitter disputes between the outgoing de Klerk government's attempt to reify older, less progressive practices and the incoming ANC's attempt to renegotiate the new nation's public history. Control of the membership of the National Monuments Council became a central battleground, and the Truth and Reconciliation Commission also played a significant role by illuminating the crimes against humanity committed under the apartheid regime. In controversial public statements and hearings, the government announced that it would grant amnesty to anyone who admitted through oral testimony their guilt in state-sanctioned violence and oppression between 1948 and 1994. Such actions were used as a method for the nation to unify and heal under Mandela's so-called national unity government. In October 2002, the minister of education, Professor Kader Asmal, organized a conference, "History, Memory, and Human Progress," which brought together teachers, public historians, and policymakers to reflect on the many ways in which history was being studied and taught in the new South Africa, with a focus on textbooks, music, and public history sites.[23] Yet even though public history played an active role in attempts to confront and heal the nation's collective memory, difficulties remain. For instance, in 2012, commemorations around the two hundredth anniversary of the settlement of Grahamstown were a reminder of the disparate views of the past that continue into the present. In Grahamstown, debate centered on whether the commemorations should be called a celebration, if conducting any activities would "be giving unwarranted attention to Col. Graham, the butcher," and if the anniversary would detract from the ANC's own hundredth-anniversary celebrations.[24] Still, racial apartheid in South Africa, while contested, has been addressed and approached more quickly than it is has in the United States, in large part because of the political marginalization of the National Party, the presence of a black majority that had been subjugated under apartheid, and very public debates about the renegotiation of the nation's past and its public presentation.

The historian David Blight reminds us that, "[i]n the wake of the [U.S.] Civil War [1861–65], there were no 'Truth and Reconciliation' commissions through which to process memories of either slavery or the experience of total war."[25] Blight's seminal work on the fracturing of collective memory in the fifty years after the war and the end of slavery convincingly shows that many white Americans favored reunion and the resubjugation of African Americans over racial justice and emancipation. Thus, the Lost Cause narrative, which presented slavery as a benign institution and remembered the war as the shared suffering of valiant (white) soldiers on both sides, came to dominate southern and U.S. history. The Lost Cause's long legacy relegated

African Americans to second-class-citizen status and significantly silenced their histories until the mid-twentieth century, when the rise of the civil rights movement and the introduction of what became known as the new social history began challenging the nation's deeply ingrained, unequal, historical narratives of race. In 1961, the centennial year of the Civil War, the civil rights movement was just gathering momentum, yet in the south "the Civil War remained unfinished."[26] During the 1960s and 1970s, for instance, southern heritage groups and National Parks staff clashed over suggestions to broaden the interpretation at Harper's Ferry National Park to include African American history. As the southern historian W. Fitzhugh Brundage writes, "[t]he civic landscape of the South looks the way it does because of both persistent inequality etched and erected in public spaces and dogged efforts to revise the same terrain."[27]

Such erasures gradually changed as African Americans gained more economic and political power after World War II, especially with the passage of the Civil Rights Act of 1964 and the Voting Rights Act of 1965. The founding of African American community and neighborhood museums were early signs of the movement's challenge to white power, for these institutions offered counterhegemonic challenges that inserted African American history and culture into the public sphere. The creators of the DuSable Museum of African American History in Chicago (founded in 1961), the International Afro-American Museum in Detroit (founded in 1965), and the Anacostia Community Museum in Washington, DC (founded in 1967) understood the political and social power of their institutions and drew explicit connections to the black power movement. Margaret Burroughs, who led the DuSable Museum, argued that these museums "emerged as the culmination of the spaces carved out by generations of local black community organizations." And because the institutions and their communities were grounded in the politics and ideology of the black power movement, their supporters saw them as not only challenges to the traditional "temples of Euro-American hegemony" but also as communicators of "a radical new agenda about power, memory, and identity." Approaches to representing African American history became even more diverse during the 1980s and 1990s, when a second wave of black public-history influenced the creation of more civil rights museums and related public history sites.[28]

Interpretations of slavery have changed rapidly at public history sites throughout the United States. At the Liberty Bell Center at Independence National Historic Park, archeological efforts inspired the inclusion of slavery into stories of the nation's founding. At Monticello, tours now feature Sally Hemings, an enslaved woman with whom Thomas Jefferson had children. A controversy over the *Back of the Big House* exhibit at the Library of Congress led public historians to make further attempts to address the historical erasure of African American history from the nation's historical sites, monuments, and museums.[29] As in the South African context, these new interpretations have provoked backlash, mostly from white Americans, who feel that "their" history is being threatened.

Across the south, interpreters of slavery are working to acknowledge African American history and culture more broadly, and a number of museums and historic sites are now dedicated to honoring the civil rights movement. At least fifteen such museums have opened in the United States since 1990. A 2008 survey by the Association of African American Museums identified more than 150 museums that were "actively curating some aspect of black history . . . from [the] A. Philip Randolph Pullman Porter Museum in Chicago to the W. C. Handy Home and Museum in Florence, Alabama, honoring the famed blues artist." Although these museums have attempted to correct the silences and erasures of African Americans and have assumed "a central place in American historical memory," they take divergent approaches to the task, and disagreements about interpretation, especially of the civil rights movement, have emerged.[30]

Some of these sites take a "consensus memory" approach to the movement: one that begins in the mid-1950s, ends with the assassination of Martin Luther King, Jr., and emphasizes southern U.S. history. They include a number of institutions that are centrally concerned with the great men of the era—notably, King. The National Park Service oversees the Martin Luther King, Jr., National Historical Park in Atlanta, which was founded on October 10, 1980, to "protect and interpret for the benefit, inspiration, and education of present and future generations the places where . . . King . . . was born, where he lived, worked, and worshipped, and where he is buried." Information on the website situates his life within the physical landscape of the site and places him at the center of the civil rights movement:

> The assassination of Martin Luther King, Jr., in Memphis, Tennessee, on April 4, 1968, robbed the American Civil Rights Movement of one of its most effective and respected leaders. Following his death, SCLC [the Southern Christian Leadership Conference] and other black activist organizations continued civil protests. But these organizations' beliefs and tactics varied widely, and their subsequent campaigns never gained the cohesion which, although fragile at times, generally characterized the progressive campaigns led by King.[31]

Other institutions take a different approach—among them BCRI. Since its founding in 1992, it has attempted to situate itself and Birmingham's civil rights history within a broader historiographical and international human rights context. Speaking at its opening, Andrew Young, once the U.S. ambassador to the United States and a former executive director of the Southern Christian Leadership Conference, declared, "When I saw the Berlin Wall come down, when I saw the students in Tiananmen Square, when I saw the Polish shipyard workers and when they all were singing 'We Shall Overcome,' I kn[e]w that what we did in Birmingham not only had an impact on human rights in the South of the United States, but really made an impact on the entire world."[32] Much of BCRI's early programming, including its human rights gallery and its celebrations of Martin Luther King, Jr., Day, "aimed at broadening the scope of the visitor experience beyond Birmingham."[33] Odessa Woolfolk, the institution's founding board chair, acknowledged these international connections: "From its inception the Institute founders recognized the universality of human conflict. After all, Dr. Martin L. King had been deeply influenced by the religious and ethnic conflicts in India, parts of Africa and Eastern Europe earlier in the twentieth century. In time these and other nations drew positive lessons from the American Civil Rights Movement. Given this broad historical context, the Institute perceived human rights as a universal striving."[34]

This international relationship drew on a long history of connections between Birmingham and Johannesburg as well as parallels between the structurally racist governmental policies in both of their nations. Historical associations between these communities were so strong that Birmingham "came to be known, in later years, as America's Johannesburg."[35] This link was also emphasized by the U.S. civil rights leader Joseph Lowery, who said in a 2007 interview that "Birmingham was probably the Johannesburg of the South. Apartheid was at its severest in Birmingham. And [Birmingham civil rights activist] Fred Shuttlesworth was the man for the hour." Nelson Mandela, during a visit to Atlanta in 1990, told Birmingham city officials that while he was imprisoned on Robben Island he drew strength from 1963 media images of Birmingham's moment.[36]

The historic ties between these two sites were central to "The International Youth Legacy Project." In the preamble to the Museums Connect grant application, the authors emphasized that youth participants from minority schools in these communities would take part in activities "designed to increase knowledge and understanding of the parallels between the civil rights movement in Birmingham and the anti-apartheid struggle in Soweto, the dynamic role of museums in interpreting those struggles, and the implications for citizens today." In making the case for the grant, Pijeaux explained, "For some time we have desired to collaborate with a partner outside the United States and particularly in South Africa, a place with which Birmingham, Alabama, shares experiences that make it ripe for comparative study and analysis by our youth and visiting public."[37]

EXPLORING PARALLEL HISTORIES

The project was delayed by difficulties connected to the Mandela House Museum. Thus, without time to train students in oral history methodologies, the facilitators had to abandon the planned oral history portion of the grant: "to collect and preserve intangible cultural heritage through oral interviews and movement music." The central activities of the grant became a concurrent study of the two countries' histories, each team's travel to the other's country, and a community celebration in each city during the students' visits. The study sessions, which, according to the proposal, were "just as important as travel to one another's country," included readings, discussions, films, debates, and field trips to other sites. Both museums hosted these sessions for their students. Readings included scholarship such as Andrew Manis's *A Fire You Can't Put Out:*

The Civil Rights Life of Birmingham's Reverend Fred Shuttlesworth, Horace Huntley and John W. McKerley's *Foot Soldiers for Democracy: The Men, Women, and Children of Birmingham,* and the autobiographies of Nelson Mandela (*Long Walk to Freedom*) and Steve Biko (*I Write What I Like*). After reading, discussing, and debating these books via weekly study sessions and Skype conversations with their international colleagues, the students watched and discussed four films: *Sarafina!* (1992), *Amandla! A Revolution in Four-Part Harmony* (2002), *4 Little Girls* (1997), and *Mighty Times: The Children's March* (2004). In addition, the Birmingham students attended public showings of the seven-part documentary *Have You Heard from Johannesburg?* (2010).[38]

According to Anderson, this shared exploration of the two communities' parallel histories created a rich avenue for discussion. In the grant report, she recalled one particular Skype session: "With a television camera rolling, ten students gathered in the Resource Gallery of the [BCRI] to talk with ten fellow teenagers gathered at the U.S. Consulate in Johannesburg, South Africa . . . After discussing similarities between the civil rights movement in the U.S. and the anti-Apartheid Movement in South Africa, the students quizzed each other about popular music."[39] Even allowing for what might have been an overly positive interpretation for the grant report, her anecdotal observations suggest that the shared historical exploration encouraged empathy and connection building.

Andrew Cedar, a senior advisor in DOS's Office of the Under Secretary of Public Diplomacy and Public Affairs, observed a Skype session between Birmingham and Soweto students while traveling in South Africa in May 2011. He called it "a fascinating example of . . . people-to-people exchange." Cedar continued: "Listening to these students exchange views on everything from race relations in their communities to Nicki Minaj demonstrated the power of readily-available technology to build bridges across oceans and cultures."[40] To him, it was an example of "the U.S. government inviting citizens into honest dialogue." In other words, differing from Anderson, who focused on shared discussions of the two communities' histories, Cedar focused on the popular-culture conversations that suggested affinity among the students. The project, like others discussed in this book, reflected the compatibility between dialogic museum programming and the DOS mission of people-to-people public diplomacy.

Both groups of students visited their communities' historic sites, by themselves and with their overseas partners. Along with the other activities, this was an attempt to lead participants toward a more complex understanding of their own histories and a more sophisticated view of the similarities between their countries' histories. The goal was to move beyond great-men interpretations and explore "the role of youth in these two movements for social change."[41] The Apartheid Museum's weekly study sessions centered on the black consciousness movement led by Biko, whose work formed much of the grassroots protest and opposition to the apartheid regime and inspired the Soweto youth uprising in 1976. In their email responses, Masiza and Davy emphasized his importance in South Africa's anti-apartheid history. Participants also studied Mandela's role, but, as Davy explained, "[his] story was told as part of the general apartheid history and of course his leadership." Unlike the Birmingham students, who had already graduated from BCRI's "Legacy Youth Leadership" program and knew a great deal about U.S. civil rights history, the students in South Africa were unfamiliar with the details of the struggle in either country. Davy said, "We were shocked to discover that our students had very little knowledge of their own history and even less of the civil rights movement. We had to start from scratch, teaching them the apartheid story and later the civil rights movement."[42] Despite this knowledge differential, the South African students were able to move beyond the dominant figures of their history and begin to see the larger historical context.

By exploring the international similarities, the South African students learned a more complex story than they would have if they had studied only their own history. This work gave them an understanding of the anti-apartheid movement that was deeper than the version available in their school curriculum or in popular culture. Masiza said, "It was very interesting for our students to learn about the similarities in the shared historical struggles. For them it was an opportunity to learn comprehensively about their struggle icons. The curriculum does not cover Steve Biko and Mandela as much as it should . . . This project gave them a wealth of knowledge as they were able to shine in the classroom and were also able to share the knowledge with fellow students."[43] The Soweto students agreed. Miriam, for example, recalled:

> During the project we learnt the differences that were faced by black people living in South Africa. South Africans were discriminated [against] merely because of their different skin colour. We also learnt that one of many reasons that triggered the marches by students in Soweto during 1976 (which was a turning point for South Africa) was the students were forced to learn in Afrikaans as a medium of instruction; other reasons were that black people were forced to carry a dompas [internal passport] wherever they went. Black people were not allowed to share food, bars, sport areas, restaurants and toilets with white people. The black people were not even allowed to get married to a person outside their race or even should live near the white people. Through all of those different projects and movements such as the Black Consciousness were established, that taught black people to be proud of who they are, to embrace their difference and accept them, to stop feeling inferior to the whites.
>
> The American Civil Rights Movement was not that different to the Apartheid system; both countries faced the same treatments. Whites were more privileged than African Americans. We learnt that the goals of the civil rights movement were to end racial segregation through non-violent protests. Although there were boycotts such as the bus boycott, which took place in Montgomery, Alabama, when Rosa Parks refused to give up her seat to a white person. During the project we discovered that both movements used secret places such as churches to hold private meetings and discuss how they were going to try and end the segregation.[44]

Soweto student Lesedi differed with Miriam's conclusion that the movements were "not that different": "The slight difference would be that American history had much more religious leaders who were against the segregation as compared to South Africa."[45]

BCRI's study sessions also explored the similarities and differences between the communities' histories and the complex layers of participation in the two movements. However, the sessions in Birmingham built upon the strong base of knowledge that the students already possessed, developing and extending it in a comparative context. Instructor Barry McNealy recalled, "[I]t wasn't a whole lot of a leap to apply what they [had] learned already to another [geographical] setting." According to Craig, the students' parallel explorations revealed similarities between their countries' and communities' struggles against racial apartheid but also highlighted some nuanced differences. For instance, the Birmingham students learned that their counterparts' histories were "in some ways more horrible over there than they were here." Like the South African students, the U.S. participants felt that the study sessions met the grant's goals to "increase knowledge and understanding of the parallels between the civil rights movement in Birmingham and the anti-apartheid struggle in Soweto." One of them, Michael, recalled, "I learned the true legacy of white supremacy and the power of unity . . . yet unity of all helped rid the injustices of the segregationist." Another, Jhana Plump, saw differences between the two countries' historical experiences: "The kids here were beaten with batons and water hoses, but, in South Africa, you would be shot. It was much more gruesome."[46] Such reflections and analyses, however, did not extend to discussions of contemporary similarities and differences.

ACTIVATING SITES OF CONSCIENCE

Both the Apartheid Museum's and BCRI were members of the International Coalition of Sites of Conscience (ICSC). In keeping with both organization's mission, a central goal of the Museums Connect project was "to develop young people as leaders" and to use history as a way to "examine the implications for contemporary society." This goal fit with the ICSC's commitment to activating "the power of places of memory to engage the public in connecting past and present in order to envision and shape a more just and humane future." In the words of the public historian Graham Black, museums should show "local people and communities the importance of having an active role in decision-making for the future."[47]

During their trip to Alabama, the South African students visited a number of sites connected to the civil rights movement in order to better understand the role and experiences of young people during historic events at sites of segregation. Ward explained, "To come here, specifically to Birmingham, was big for them . . . And then they come here and see how many parallels there were and to go through the [Sixteenth Street Baptist] church and have the opportunity to go through the [Kelly Ingram] park. I think it was big. And we went to Selma and Montgomery and walked across that [Edmund Pettus] bridge." Similarly, when the U.S. delegation traveled to South Africa, the students visited many of Johannesburg's sites of conscience and met veterans of the 1976 Soweto uprising. In conjunction with the Apartheid Museum's community celebration of International Youth Day, they explored at length the role of youth in the anti-apartheid movement. After visiting Regina Mundi Church, Constitution Hill, and Market Theatre, in addition to the Voortrekker Monument, the Apartheid Museum, and the Mandela House Museum, the U.S. students gained a deeper understanding of the anti-apartheid movement and were able to reflect on the complex similarities and differences between Johannesburg and Birmingham. McNealy recalled that only by visiting each other's countries and historic sites and meeting young people from those places could the students develop a full understanding of the communities' shared suffering. Speaking of the American participants, he said, "Ultimately the trip there to Johannesburg, I believe, solidified in their minds how international the idea of discrimination and segregation was . . . I think that when they were able to take it out of a textbook and talk to another human being who had experiences and ideas and a reference frame from which they could discuss it, I think it just made it much more powerful."[48]

Many of the project facilitators and all of the students reported that one particular event was a defining moment during the year-long project: hearing U.S. First Lady Michelle Obama "speak to young leaders about their role in promoting change" at the historic Regina Mundi Church on Youth Day. The event, organized by the U.S. Consulate, combined the power of fame with a symbol of historical injustice. Davy, who gave Mrs. Obama a tour of the Apartheid Museum during her visit, recalled, "We queued for hours in what was probably the coldest morning in Johannesburg, before we got into the venue to listen to Mrs. Obama speak. [It was a] big highlight for all!" McNealy recalled that both groups of students were "transfixed" by Mrs. Obama's remarks.[49]

In his final evaluation, American student Brandon wrote, "The project broadened my knowledge of African history and allowed me to build friendships with youth from South Africa. We also engaged in discussions about solving problems for the future. This was the best thing that ever happened to me." These discussions, South African student Lesedi recalled, also gave students the rare opportunity to connect their historical knowledge with current racial intolerance and injustice: "When we discuss[ed] about it, it all becomes emotional to imagine the pain that other people went through for us to be free. In all that we have learnt to embrace the colour of our skin and the freedom that we have."[50]

The Apartheid Museum's staff said that using the past as a way to talk and learn about social justice issues in South Africa was an important goal for the collaboration. According to Masiza, learning about the parallels between the two movements and visiting historic sites in both countries was especially valuable for the Soweto students, many of whom had never left their part of Johannesburg: "[It] made our kids appreciate themselves, their immediate environment, their country, and their Africanness." This reflection suggests that the Museums Connect project facilitated a greater exploration of self through a deeper engagement with the past, challenging students to consider their positions as potential leaders and forces for change. Craig noted that the BCRI students' visit to South Africa and their study of the anti-apartheid movement taught them "to be less arrogant about being from the United States of America. And for them to know that there are people just like them all over the world. People are people, period. It doesn't matter where you come from." This lesson was significant. When the staff had first unveiled the project to the teens, they were peppered with queries about South African life: "Do they have roads? Do they have animals walking up and down the street?"[51] BCRI facilitator Ahmad Ward spoke of the virtue of visiting historic sites as a means of learning about a shared history: "For them [the BCRI students] to go this far away and have that kind of cultural experience . . . a lot of those kids have never been the same. They still really are affected by being over there." He recalled the group's shock and horror upon seeing bullet holes in the walls of Mandela House: "It was a very enriching experience for me as well as the kids."[52]

Yet the shortened time frame and the focus on leadership and learning about history meant that project facilitators could not instigate significant discussions about contemporary race relations. This created the unstated yet implicit conclusion that both Birmingham and Johannesburg have moved beyond deep racism since the Jim Crow and apartheid eras. This conclusion was supported by participant and facilitator interviews. With a few notable exceptions, most participants neglected to mention any discussion of race vis-à-vis the Museums Connect project. This marginalization of potentially dissonant discussions of contemporary race relations (mirroring a similar outcome in NCC and NMA's *Being We the People* project) also occurred during BCRI's Nelson Mandela Day celebration.

"HE'S JUST WHO HE IS!"

During the South African students' visit to Birmingham, BCRI hosted a brand-new community festival, Nelson Mandela Day, in adjoining Kelly Ingram Park to celebrate the project and connect the two countries' histories. "I can't describe the atmosphere in the park," said Cooper. "It was electric."[53] The festival's success in attracting new audiences was a point of pride in the reflections of all BCRI staff involved. It was also an indication of the significance of the historic connections between Birmingham and Johannesburg and the power of Mandela to inspire international audiences outside of South Africa. Anderson said, "[Mandela Day] somehow caught the attention of people who had never been here before and haven't been here since. I mean the park was full of people with all different skin colors: that's still pretty unusual, for that park or for our events. And I got so many comments from people of all different types delighting in that, and I think it had a lot to do with how people feel about Nelson Mandela too . . . He's just who he is!"[54]

A multiracial crowd of more than a thousand people attended the festival—what Cooper called "a huge community impact"—far larger and more diverse than the attendance at BCRI's annual Juneteenth festival. New corporate sponsors were tapped to support the event, which attracted them due to the festival's connection with South Africa. Among these sponsors was a South African resident of Birmingham who had invented the vuvuzela. For one day at least, BCRI was able to transcend its reputation as, in Anderson's words, the "the black museum [where] white people don't go."[55]

Like Anderson, McNealy believed that Mandela's embrace of forgiveness and his "idea of working together, instead of trying to crush his enemies" had a wide local appeal: "[In] a city like Birmingham, Alabama, with the history that it has, it's very, very important to keep the idea of moving forward and not grinding axes or settling scores and trying to move forward in unity as a community, I think, in my opinion, that's what appeals to Birminghamians about Nelson Mandela because we've seen it here, from what has taken place in the 1940s, and '50s, and '60s, to what takes place today." He concluded, "[W]hen you've lived it and see it first hand, and then to have an example, a living example at the time, such as Nelson Mandela, I just think that was . . . something that kind of called to people's better nature." McNealy's analysis mirrored larger narratives that lionized and focused on Mandela's forgiveness of his white oppressors. A global outpouring of reverence and grief followed Mandela's death in 2013. The U.S. news network CNN reflected the dominant interpretation of his life when it reported, "His message of reconciliation, not vengeance, inspired the world after he negotiated a peaceful end to segregation and urged forgiveness for the white government that imprisoned him."[56]

Student responses reflected the centrality and importance of Mandela as a figure. "Mandela, the powerful man, the hero, the role model, he should be celebrated," South African student Abongile Kala told a reporter at the Mandela Day celebration. Another South African student, Sibusiso Dube, noted, "Because the same way you celebrate here, we celebrate him the same way in South Africa."[57] Dube's comments moved beyond the festival's great man interpretation to point out historical parallels: "In the civil rights movement, Americans had to put all they've got for their freedom . . . Like in South Africa, we had to sacrifice everything . . . The youth wanted changes in their community, they were fighting for freedoms." His remarks to the reporter demonstrated his awareness of differences between the two movements, including the significance of churches and religious leaders in the United States as compared to South Africa. Anderson recalled that, throughout the celebration, including during the formal remarks that concluded the day, the students sought to educate the larger public about the connections between the two communities and their iconic leaders.[58] It is difficult to know how successful the participants were in this endeavor, but McNealy was optimistic: "I'm sure people left with a greater knowledge of the story of South Africa and its connection to the history of Birmingham and the Jim Crow south.

I'm sure they left with an appreciation of that connection, but then they also got the chance to come out and celebrate a public space, which was enjoyable." The presence of both countries' students on stage, listening to and singing songs associated with both movements alongside some of the original Birmingham activists, suggest that this was possible.[59]

The public's engagement with this history is much less certain, given that Mandela Day was a one-time event. According to staff members, the community has not responded similarly to subsequent BCRI programming, so it is unclear if the public has moved beyond the great man interpretation of Mandela as an international figure of peace. His appeal in Birmingham fits into Owen J. Dwyer's analysis of the "emphasis on individual greatness and dramatic events" that attracts "visitors in an entertainment market saturated with the spectacular and hyperreal." Dwyer argues that a larger focus on international human rights, such as that undertaken by BCRI and the National Civil Rights Museum in Memphis, "shifts attention away from the contemporary and local towards the spectacular and global." This analysis can be extrapolated to BCRI's success in attracting a diverse public to their Mandela Day celebration. It is possible that the event felt safe and comfortable for a city in which politics are still wrapped in the complexities of race.[60]

All of the BCRI staff involved with the Museums Connect project lamented the institute's inability to replicate the public excitement that the Mandela Day program created. This outcome, similar to issues of sustainability discussed in chapters 2 and 3, contradicted their goal of serving diverse community audiences. As the public historian Mindy Duitz argues, "[it] is critical that all museums realize that serving their communities does not mean just a seasonal program or an annual exhibition in the 'community gallery.' It is an ongoing activity that requires clear policy and sufficient resources. It is also a reflection of an institution's mission and its vision of its role as a public educational institution."[61] In this case, both BCRI and the Apartheid Museum lacked "clear policy and sufficient resources" beyond this Museums Connect project. Still, moments of vibrant, spontaneous, yet difficult-to-quantify community engagements did occur when each museum's team traveled to the other's country.

For instance, while exploring Birmingham during a break in scheduled activities, Masiza met two local community activists: coffeeshop owners Yvonne Thomas and Yvette Chatman (who was also BCRI parent educator and curriculum facilitator). Masiza recalled that they "and other ladies [were] having a discussion in a community where literacy was taught to homeless people and [about] all the projects done in that small environment." She recalled this encounter with joy, saying that it was one of the highlights of her time in the United States because it allowed for genuine dialogue and community exploration. Chatman similarly recalled the power of short conversations and the quick relationships that developed during Masiza's visit: "They were so full of laughter. Jacquie [Masiza] said that the shop was full of Ubuntu, a South African philosophy that loosely means 'humanness, connectiveness, and 'I am because you are.' I thanked her and promised that I would use that term whenever I talked about my business." Chatman concluded, "It was really wonderful to meet [Masiza and Davy] . . . It's always a pleasure to meet someone that has made a difference in your living, and life. I am better for meeting the two of them." The passion of Masiza's and Chatman's responses suggests that Museums Connect projects were able to foster spontaneous moments of encounter and engagement by facilitating participants' exposure to each other's community.[62] While hard to quantify, this seemed to have had positive effects on both of the museums and their community members. It certainly exemplified DOS's people-to-people diplomacy and showed the potential to further BCRI's standing in the eyes of a wider public. And by connecting this wider public with South Africa and the Apartheid Museum, it highlighted the project's potential to forge deeper, longer-lasting community bonds.

"WOW! I'M IN AFRICA!": REFLECTION IN ACTION

Unlike the museum partners discussed in chapters 2 and 3, BCRI and the Apartheid Museum had a relatively equitable relationship. This was made clear in their shared histories, their relative size and scope, and their institutional cultures. Although BCRI was officially the lead museum, its staff was willing to be reflective and did not presume that it had more expertise than the Apartheid Museum staff did. The involvement of local Birmingham community members further reduced the power differential between the two museums and contributed to a sense of shared exploration. Staff from both museums agreed that the BCRI facilitators did not see themselves as the experts: they were all learning together. This approach had the unintended result of making a deep personal and professional impact on the project facilitators, who recalled that they often felt as if they were learning as much as their students were.

Many BCRI staff reported that working on this comparative transnational project expanded their knowledge of and perspectives on their shared histories. Ward said,

> I think that once you get past the whole thing of "Wow! I'm in Africa!" which was big for me. Every night I used to stand there like "Wow, I'm in Africa!" It's a place where I've always wanted to go and "I'm here," that needs to not be understated. Well, once you get past that it was really about the history for me. I think I'm always looking at ways that I can tie it, I do a lot of talking for the Institute, that's one of the things that I do, and I do a lot of programming, and it just helped me to really get a handle on the human rights aspect of this . . . And I think it has helped me to expand my knowledge base in a way that I think I'm doing a better job of describing what the power of segregation was. And how it was necessary to end it.[63]

His openness to new experiences and perspectives and his willingness to place himself in the position of fellow student alongside the school-aged participants were clear in his description of his emotional responses to the visit: "'Wow, we are actually here!' And, [co-facilitator] Barry [McNealy] and I have been friends for a long time, so we had this experience like I felt like I was at home. Most of the people that met us over the first couple of days were like 'Welcome home, brother!' And, wow, that is something. And especially if you are a young black male—to be in the area where for the first time in your life you're in a majority . . . I've never had that experience before. It was powerful."[64]

Ward's enthusiasm was matched by Cooper's. Although she was not involved in the day-to-day operations of the grant, she nonetheless reflected on the virtues of working collaboratively with like-minded colleagues in South Africa: "To work with museum professionals in another country was very professionally rewarding. I think, the big piece being, being able to work through the potential problem and to collaboratively come up with solutions on how we were going to make it happen . . . [T]hat was great." Like Ward, Cooper embraced the role of facilitator rather than knowledge giver as she acknowledged how much she learned throughout the year-long project: "[B]ecause I am actually a student of African history and culture, . . . to have that experience was both personally and professionally rewarding."[65]

The Birmingham team was willing to admit their ignorance about South Africa and confess to limitations in their professional understandings and practice. This led them to welcome knowledgeable community members into the project. Nonhlanhla Jones, a South African woman who lived in Birmingham, became a volunteer mentor to BCRI students as they learned about the two countries' histories. In addition to talking with them about apartheid and the anti-apartheid movement, she helped prepare Ward, McNealy, and Craig to take the students to Johannesburg. BCRI embraced such new community voices in its programming, and during interviews a number of facilitators mentioned Jones's involvement and expertise. Anderson said, "She's like one of the staff almost." Since the end of the project, Jones has remained engaged with BCRI as a community supporter and advocate as well as an unofficial mentor and facilitator of its youth programs, in contrast to the community members who were attracted only to BCRI's Mandela Day celebration.[66]

Staff interviews frequently mentioned the high level of cooperation between the two museum teams as well as the deep personal friendships that evolved out of their shared inquiry. Masiza recalled, "My birthday fell on the day of our departure [back to South Africa] and everyone made a big deal of it. It was what we call the Spirit of Ubuntu (human kindness) in South Africa, and Barry's [McNealy's] wife made a caramel cake for me, my favorite, and I got gifts."[67] Although they were officially the lead team, BCRI staff were willing to share control of the project activities with their South African colleagues, even though a significant differential existed between BCRI's and the Apartheid Museum's programmatic capacities. As a result, the Museums Connect project became a vehicle for institutional change. Learning from BCRI's already-existing "Legacy Youth Leadership" program, the Apartheid Museum team developed a new method of community youth engagement. Davy said, "On a professional level, [we had] a similar feeling of pride and sense of achievement that through the auspices of the museum, we were able to achieve a successful intervention and project. We really need to do it on an annual basis so that more students can be impacted." Masiza said that seeing the work BCRI did with students in its own community helped her understand "how museums work in other countries."[68]

In other words, unlike more nefarious practices that might be exported through a program such as Museums Connect, the exchange of ideas regarding museums and community engagement was seen as a positive development among the Apartheid Museum staff rather than a sinister foreign imposition. Both Masiza and Davy lamented their financial inability to continue this method of engagement. Masiza said, "I managed to help the youth from my community achieve their full potential in life. I built a very good relationship with the students, which are still going strong. I still learn so much from them, and I am humbled by their gratitude for the role I played in their lives . . . [E]very milestone in their lives is shared, and I get teary every time!" Davy suggested that the type of engagement enacted during the project could act as a catalyst for the Apartheid Museum to begin more community programs: "On a personal level, I have a sense of pride and feel a bit like a Big Mama! To see the students excelling as they are, knowing that the program has much to do with it, makes me proud and fills me with a need to do more."[69]

Michele Peregrin of DOS applauded this successful transmission of U.S. professional museum practices within an international partnership. Yet unlike Cedar, whose recollections of the students' Skype conversations focused only on their people-to-people conversations, she was also impressed by the subsequent work that both groups had done:

> I heard about the impact that Museums Connect has had on its alumni. A museum team from the Apartheid Museum in South Africa was so impressed by the Birmingham Institute['s] . . . inclusion of high school volunteers in its activities and operations that they decided to launch their very first volunteer program, with the Museums Connect participants as its first cohort, upon their return. Almost a year after this exchange took place, I learned that the South African students not only continue to volunteer, but were so inspired by their trip to Alabama that they are now focused on actively pursuing scholarships to study in the United States.[70]

While Peregrin's comments may have been influenced by her need to emphasize the grant's impact in her final report, they nonetheless highlighted her celebration of the museums' exchange of ideas, with special emphasis on the impact of BCRI on the Apartheid Museum. This outcome exemplified a larger shift in U.S. public diplomacy that placed exchange and dialogue at the center and acknowledged the non-U.S. participants' decision-making agency rather than encouraged U.S. citizens to overtly sell American ideas and culture.

PRODUCING YOUTH LEADERS?

Within similar historical and public history contexts, the BCRI and its two South African partners successfully overcame early challenges and engaged their student teams in a shared exploration of both countries' histories and connections. Including the Apartheid Museum in the project not only helped facilitators move beyond the movements' great men to explore deeper complexities but also added an institution that in size and interpretive scope more closely resembled BCRI. The willingness of BCRI staff to collaborate with rather than dominate their South African counterparts contributed to the collegial environment.[71] In addition, BCRI's capacity to engage in youth programs drove the form of the grant and challenged the Apartheid Museum to begin its own youth program, a point that both the South African museum professionals and DOS officials celebrated.

The central grant activity involved students' weekly study sessions and visits to historic sites of conscience. Although they engaged in a deep shared exploration of their communities' histories, constraints such as time, subject-matter complexity, and a focus on leadership mostly prevented the students from shifting their conversations to contemporary issues of race. The Mandela Day celebration in Birmingham emphasized the different impact of the grant on two publics: the participating students versus the larger community of Birmingham, who for a few hours came together to celebrate Nelson Mandela. However, spontaneous moments of encounter between Apartheid Museum staff and Birmingham community members suggest another model for engaging a wider public beyond the narrow circle of students at the center of the Museums Connect project.

As with the other case studies explored in this book, this one-time funding opportunity precluded a sustained, long-term engagement with these new publics. Cooper acknowledged these challenges from BCRI's perspective. Eighteen months after the grant ended she recalled, "We've been able to continue the relationship with other funding, but those kids would love to come back, and our kids would love to go back. Some of them have questions about trying to come here to school and college. Being able to get tied in to other resources once a project is over, that would be very helpful." Yet she said, "It's given us a model for how we may look at building other international collaborations," a significant outcome for a museum that self-reflectively struggled to "activate its international mission" before the grant award. Still, she had to acknowledge that "money and staff resources, those are the challenges." Ward noted that since the project ended "we get a lot of requests if we're going to do it again. People [the broader public] asking us if we'll do it again, and it all depends on money, obviously. If the opportunity opened itself again, I don't think we'd hesitate to try and do it again." BCRI, however, has not continued to engage with the same partners and create a level of community excitement similar to Mandela Day, and the project has not been replicated.[72]

The Apartheid Museum staff also highlighted the challenges of sustainability. Davy said that the Museums Connect partnership "fulfill[ed] one of the key objectives of the museum, which is partnerships with other similar institutions to spread the word of reconciliation and peace." Yet "I wish we had more [money] as there is so much to do, learn and share. The continuation of the program and the consistency is of vital importance." Masiza felt a sense of urgency to continue the work begun during the project, "[e]ven if we don't take kids to the U.S. but have joint programs to keep the project alive. We have produced Youth Leaders and possibly future country leadership and they need to share their experiences and to impart the knowledge to the next group."[73]

While the two institutions have not been able to develop a sustainable long-term relationship beyond personal friendships and exchange of correspondence (as in the case studies analyzed in chapters 2 and 3), some of the student participants have extended the work they began during the project. In 2012 a number of the Birmingham students and one of the South African students participated in the eleventh annual Birmingham Teen Pledge Conference. Here they not only reflected on their Museums Connect experience in a session that they organized and hosted called "International Stereotypes" but also were able to speak personally about overcoming stereotyping and intolerance through their connection to the museums and by activating the memory of the civil rights and anti-apartheid movements.[74]

Both museums' staff speculated that the project had empowered several of the students to become leaders and advocates for the museums. Davy mused, "This project was the catalyst for them to pursue their leadership qualities in a far more informed manner. They realized that there was a bigger world out there and most of them are now at university, or distance learning [and] working at the same time. We believe that the program enabled their own thinking about their lives, dreams, and potential. A few of them have really grabbed their opportunities and are running with it." Likewise, Masiza said, "Our students are excelling in their chosen fields . . . [T]he sky is the limit . . . [A]nything is possible. They are now leaders at college and are involved in leadership programs to enhance that skill . . . A quest for learning and future leadership was extended." She hoped that these young people would not squander the opportunity to effect change in their community: "We have produced youth leaders and possibly future country leadership, and they need to share their experiences and then impart the knowledge to the next group." Anderson believed that both museums gained advocates and supporters from the students and their friends and families: "These same students also serve as docents at BCRI, incorporating their experiences and knowledge of South Africa's history into comments they offer visitors as they guide them through the Human Rights Gallery." Craig paraphrased a South African student who had been interviewed in Birmingham: "It makes me inspired to know that I can go back home and go to the Apartheid Museum of the Mandela House and do the same thing, I want to do what they do [e.g., give tours]."[75]

CONCLUSION

From the beginning, institutions participating in the Museums Connect program struggled to navigate through the tensions of a program that had hierarchies of power built into its foundational structure. Despite the confluence of immediate factors, the program was the convergence of two paradigms—public history's late-twentieth-century democratic approach to history making and DOS's people-to-people diplomacy—motivated by different desired outcomes: public history's sharing and divestiture of authority versus public diplomacy's influence and persuasion.

When museum projects are principally sponsored by the U.S. government with the purpose of furthering U.S. interests abroad, there cannot be true balance or equitable distribution of authority between the two sides of the partnership, however soft the methods of persuasion might be. Museums Connect reflected a trend among American history museums: the assumption that the authority for history making is theirs to share with communities. Thus, they privilege "giving community members more say in what stories the museum showcases and how they get told" and work to engage the knowledge and expertise of the public and communities while decentering the authoritative voice of the curator.[1] Although AAM administered the Museums Connect program and the museums were left alone before and during the project, there were clear hierarchies that favored the U.S. institutions, and these informed how the program and its projects would function. These differentials were created and informed by the specific structures of Museums Connect, including DOS's role as the program's main sponsor, its involvement in dictating the audiences for the program, its emphasis on marginalized and historically powerless communities, its interest in the geographic areas most likely to receive funding, and its requirement that the American lead museum control the financial and administrative aspects of the grant.

Museums Connect perpetuated historic hierarchies of power. The use of American English as both the bureaucratic language of the grants and the language of communication and practice among the participants reinforced inequalities linked to the global spread of the language through the British Empire and its legacy as a lingua franca. In each of the case studies in this book, the non-U.S. museum staff and community partners had to collaborate in a language other than their mother tongue. Unlike their U.S. partners, they navigated and negotiated language differences throughout the project activities. Thus, they had to operate within a programmatic paradigm that foundationally favored the U.S. museums and their community partners.

APPROACHING DISTRIBUTIONS OF POWER

The three case studies in this book revealed a variety of factors that promoted or precluded equitable power dynamics in transnational public history projects. These factors emerged from the specific local, institutional, and personal contexts that shaped each museum and participant. Not only did they highlight the heterogeneity of the museum field, but they also demonstrated both deliberate and accidental attempts to mitigate the power differentials ingrained in the structure of the Museums Connect program. In the United States, despite some innovative school instruction methods, the adult is still usually the teacher, the young person the student. Thus, the DOS's insistence that these grants should target youth communities meant that the relationships between the museums and their students were often unequal, as the case studies have shown. Only at Marefat High School did relationships among school staff members, students, and project facilitators resemble a shared inquiry, thanks to the school's focus on civic education and student empowerment and project director Jeff Stern's biases toward the school and its Hazara population. As a result, students were able to guide the terms of the dialogue during their trip to the United States and their exhibition at the National Museum of Afghanistan. In contrast, the NCC facilitators' influence over their students led to the effacement of their minority status, in keeping with the center's normative and celebratory narratives of U.S. pluralism. This didactic teaching environment was reflected in the other two case studies. Although BCRI and Apartheid Museum staff learned alongside their students, the instruction remained hierarchical because it was delivered by the staff rather than by the students. That approach was mirrored in the two projects between MHHE and BMCM. Although these museums worked with slightly older undergraduate and graduate students, the projects were framed as a vehicle for public history pedagogy, which created the conditions for didactic instruction that impeded power sharing between the museums and the students. In a special issue of the *Public History Review*, the Chinese public historian Na Li reflected on some of the pitfalls that arise when working in an international context: "While collaboration is a regular component of public history programs, going global poses further challenges . . . [D]ifferent pedagogic philosophies make some basic assumptions in our field not so basic. Sharing authority, for example, does not come easily in classrooms that have long been dominated by one authoritative voice."[2]

Age-related hierarchies in education were not the only element that affected power dynamics during these projects. Museums Connect was a public diplomacy program, formed with the intention of building affinity, promoting consensus, and celebrating commonalities between participants and museums. This approach stands in contrast to another significant mode of transnational public history, one exemplified by the International Coalition of Sites of Conscience. As discussed in chapter 4, the ICSC is a group of "sites, individuals, and initiatives" that use dialogue to activate "the power of places of memory to engage in connecting past and present in order to envision and shape a more just and humane future." Since 1999, ICSC has created global links among historic sites of trauma and memory. Its members seek to uncover dissonant and traumatic historical narratives of injustice with the intention of "transforming places that preserve the past into dynamic spaces that promote civic action on today's struggles for human rights and justice." In this way, ICSC has sought to launch transnational conversations about the present that arise from a deeper understanding of the past, including the importance of reconciliation, preventing historical erasure, and engaging in complex dialogue rather than interpreting reductive narratives about particular sites.[3] ICSC and its sites and programming are engaged in public history pursuits that use dialogue to disrupt dominant interpretations of the past, leading to action that wrestles with the contemporary legacy of historical injustices.

These two modes of transnational public history were combined in the case study discussed in chapter 4, in which two members of ICSC (BCRI and the Apartheid Museum) partnered to interrogate the counter-hegemonic narratives of racial apartheid in their respective countries. Yet the project, under the auspices of Museums Connect, was generally reconciliatory, mostly avoiding difficult discussions of contemporary race relations in favor of historical explorations. The unstated yet implicit conclusion was that the communities' greatly improved race relations were powerful enough to efface any deep discussion of contemporary racial issues in the United States or South Africa.

As their membership in ICSC indicates, BCRI and the Apartheid Museum shared an interpretive approach to their countries' histories. Combined with their parallel public history contexts, this allowed them to build a relatively equitable partnership (except in the realm of youth programming). Yet the case studies also revealed discrepancies between the ways in which history was understood and used in society as well as in how museums reflected public memory and meaning in non-U.S. and U.S. contexts. This created challenges for project activities that U.S. institutions thought would be entirely manageable. For instance, the unequal power dynamics between the NCC and NMA were exacerbated by the NMA's limited institutional capacity after decades of war as well as the museum's marginal role in Afghans' daily lives and collective memory. Despite the museum's enthusiasm for the project, it did not have the capacity to do more than serve as an exhibition space for the students' photography project. In the projects between the BMCM in Casablanca and the MHHE in Kennesaw, BMCM's local context was central to its actions throughout the grant. Museums in Morocco had a legacy of creating homogeneous national narratives to serve tourists and French colonial powers at the expense of local and marginalized Moroccans. In order to change this narrative, BMCM had to negotiate the activities of the grant to better suit the needs of its surrounding community.

Simply understanding international public history practices and museological contexts did not guarantee a shared endeavor or mitigate hierarchies and differentials between participating museums. In all three cases, the way in which U.S. museum staff approached their role as project leaders and public historians had a significant impact on the grant projects. The facilitators at BCRI and NCC responded to an urge to collaborate with their non-U.S. museum colleagues and learn alongside their student participants. As Ahmad Ward in Birmingham and Jeff Stern in Philadelphia confirmed, they recognized that public historians must reflect on and confront their own subjectivities, processes, and positions of power—including discursive power and language—when working in an international or transnational context. This is instructive for those who are also considering how to confront power differentials in a local or domestic context.[4] The relationships between the museums and their students in the Johannesburg-Birmingham and Kabul-Philadelphia projects were much more dynamic and equitable than they were in the Casablanca-Kennesaw project. Because the staff at MHHE/KSU had training and practice in formal public history methodologies, they assumed the role of expert throughout the grants, and BMCM and its students had to negotiate elements of the projects to make them function more effectively in their local context.[5]

The framing of Museums Connect grants and activities also shaped the projects. For both curators and audiences, certain types of public history activities and outcomes are easier to open to multiple interpretations and voices—for example, exhibitions designed by community participants rather than traditional interpretive text or community festivals.[6] For the MHHE and the BCMC, the creation of an online exhibition of student photographs and community oral histories became an open, multivocal way to reflect on connections between the historical and contemporary ramifications of minority Muslim identity in Morocco and Georgia. Similarly, the photography project between the NCC and the NMA ceded curatorial power to both teams of students while allowing viewers to form their own interpretations. This also had the effect of transitioning the exhibition away from a comparison of historical themes toward a contemporary discussion of societal similarities and differences. These examples reinforce the emerging argument that public historians and museum staff require a broader set of skills in order to succeed within this new museological and public history environment.[7]

In all of these projects, the idea of public historian as facilitator rather than knowledge giver was welcomed because the participating U.S. museums embraced the paradigm of the museum as forum rather than temple and elevated processes of dialogue over the development and care of a collection. Each of these relatively young institutions encouraged its staff to engage in a collaborative process in which the idea of an objective truth was marginalized in favor of multiple truths. New technological platforms aided this collaborative work, allowing closer cooperation among project participants who were physically separated by thousands of miles. Yet such approaches did not alone guarantee a balanced or reciprocal relationship. Reflecting on my analysis of the BMCM-MHHE partnership, Rebecca Conard proposed, "[H]ad there been more collaboration on the planning end, the American and Moroccan partners would have confronted early on the cultural differences over paying oral history narrators." She also noted, "Planning, of course, takes time, which is always in short supply when an application deadline is looming. But something as simple as involving all key partners in constructing the budget could at least flag issues that need further discussion before a project."[8] While the U.S. grant context is familiar to U.S. museums, non-U.S. participants are often challenged by its bureaucratic language and practices. Therefore, U.S. professionals must take great care to address assumptions around language, public history contexts, and grant practices to ensure that fundamental structures are interrogated and addressed at the beginning of transnational partnerships and collaborations. Further study of Museums Connect projects involving U.S. museums that do not wholeheartedly embrace the ideas of dialogism and the museum as forum is warranted.

In considering the multiple agencies of the different publics involved in each grant, as well as those excluded, this book provides a new forum through which to consider the assumptions of the public sphere that underlie the democratic discourse of the museum as forum and ideas of museum-community engagement.[9] Museums Connect targeted specific groups and communities in order to meet DOS's strategic goals and increase the participating museums' ability to measure the projects' effectiveness. This had the effect of including certain communities while excluding others, and the case studies highlighted conditions that both reduced and accentuated the differentials between these publics. Studying Museums Connect thus elucidates conditions that promote and preclude more or less equal power relationships between the museums and between the museums and their community partners in an international context more clearly than in a local, domestic context. And although they often operate in a local or domestic rather than a transnational context, public history practitioners can learn from these factors in attempting to engage marginalized or historically powerless communities in their own work. In the *Being We the People* project between the NCC and its students and the NMA and Marefat High school students, for example, the reflective practices of the NCC staff shrank the power differential between the Marefat students and the NCC. These exchanges allowed the students to negotiate their minority status vis-à-vis their nation while simultaneously speaking for their nation during their trip to Philadelphia. In contrast, the use of U.S. public history faculty to teach public history methodologies accentuated power differentials between the MHHE and the BMCM and required the Casablanca museum to renegotiate its local activities.

DE-CENTERING THE WEST

In moving beyond a western-centric view of museums and public history, these three Museums Connect case studies serve as a caution against generalizing about institutional and individual behavior. In each project, the participants acted, interpreted meaning, and drew conclusions based on local contexts that were rarely replicated either domestically or abroad.[10] In all cases, however, the U.S. museum professionals, in keeping with public history practice, assumed that the authority for history making, grant activities, and decision-making was theirs to share rather than an inherently collaborative endeavor. In the MHHE and BMCM projects, the power relationships were strongly in favor of the MHHE staff, who assumed the role of expert in the pedagogy activities. In the NCC-NMA project, Stern created conditions for a more equitable project dynamic, which allowed the Hazara students and the project facilitators to interpret the U.S.-created project differently from the way their colleagues in Philadelphia did. The BCRI and the Apartheid Museum interpreted their communities' histories similarly so their students came to comparable understandings of their histories.

Nancy Fraser's notion of multiple, competing, stratified, and unequal publics, developed as a western concept, was borne out in these projects.[11] Yet in each of the case studies, distinct non-U.S. memory practices, public history contexts, and competing ideas of the public sphere led the non-U.S. museums, their staff, and their community partners to challenge, translate, and negotiate the structures implemented by DOS, AAM, and the U.S. lead museums. Each of these negotiations occurred in response to specific local conditions and contexts. Nonetheless, if a public historian's goal is to engage in international or transnational partnerships and collaborations that are truly shared endeavors, western ideas about the public sphere need to be examined, challenged, and revised. Otherwise, we will continue to enact programs or projects that reflect western practices and power hierarchies and that, from the outset, disempower or disadvantage non-U.S. institutions and participants.[12]

SUSTAINABILITY AND THE FUTURE BEYOND MUSEUMS CONNECT

Because the priorities of the AAM and DOS's Bureau of Educational and Cultural Affairs had diverged, Museums Connect's final grant cycle concluded in 2017.[13] An evaluation commissioned jointly by the two organizations reported the program's "greatest takeaways" as "[l]earning about another culture," "developing meaningful relationships," "recognizing [an] institution's ability to have a wider [geographical] impact," "realizing the benefit of bringing young people together," "learning how other [non-U.S.] museums work," and "appreciating what it takes to implement an international collaboration."[14] These findings moved beyond AAM's periodic statements about the programs' outputs, such as the September 2013 tweet that claimed, "#MuseumsConnect by the numbers: 6,000 participants, more than 250,000 people reached in 33 countries & 33 U.S cities," and a 2017 video that suggested that Museums Connect "touched more than 400 community organizations and a quarter of a million people."[15] While both of these statements highlighted DOS's hoped-for ripple effect of people-to-people diplomacy and AAM's wider community goals for transnational museum collaborations, the final evaluation demonstrated that the program's greatest impact was on the participants. The impact on the institutions and wider publics was less certain.[16] Almost all of the people I interviewed concurred with AAM's final report and discussed their experiences with Museums Connect effusively and positively. The case studies in this book also highlight the program's ability to bring individuals together to form lasting relationships, the goal of DOS's people-to-people diplomacy.[17] Although individuals had diverse experiences of the program and disparate analyses of it, all spoke with fervor and enthusiasm about its ability to create deep human bonds. The opportunity to travel, meet, and work together, as well as the use of social media, email, and blogs to facilitate these relationships during and after the projects, were cited as successful approaches and results.

Yet the warmth of these recollections masked a complex public history perspective laced with subtle power dynamics.[18] This included a discordance between public diplomacy and public history's views of power as well as the absence of tangible and institutional sustainability. In each of the case studies, partners struggled to develop sustainable institutional relationships and public history activities beyond their continuing personal friendships. Even the promising work begun by the students in Soweto and Birmingham could not be sustained. Museums Connect thus more closely resembled a one-off domestic community project of the sort that are often enacted by museum professionals but lack the resources or commitment to be incorporated more completely into wider institutional practices.[19] Museums Connect created expensive projects that in all three case studies served as an extension of the institutions' existing mission but did not become a central element of that mission. The one-year timeline of each grant was too short a period to build and sustain trust and engagement with a community beyond the project's end.[20] Jennifer Dickey, in recalling the challenge of sustainability between MHHE and BMCM, noted this problem when she referred to Museums Connect funding as "seed money" that had allowed a unique project to happen outside of MHHE's everyday operations. Laura Anderson at BCRI reflected a similar sentiment when discussing the challenge of sustainability.[21]

Other observers acknowledged these challenges. Madeline Vadkerty, who replaced Heather Berry as AAM's manager of international programs in 2015, saw sustainability as a big concern: "Up until now it's been a bit hit and miss."

> One of the things that we're planning to build into future grant projects . . . is a more consistent and systematic view towards sustainability of projects. It will involve working with an organization that is focused on social entrepreneurship and connecting museums and the communities that they're working with, helping to reorient their thinking so that they can connect with their communities after the project ends. But it remains to be seen how it is going to be worked out. . . . We're adding a component to [the colloquium that all project directors attend each year] so that they will think about how to sustain their project. And hopefully that will be built into their projects in a way that will generate success in the future.[22]

Although Vadkerty's vision for building sustainability into the future of Museums Connect has not come to pass, the transnational museum-community collaborations in Museums Connect programs and the ways in which institutions and participants negotiated them are instructive. As working internationally and transnationally becomes easier, museums and public historians will continue to expand their work beyond the nation-state boundary. Moreover, as the U.S. position in international affairs alters and the global balance of power shifts, there is a vital need for a U.S.-rooted field that can constantly adjust its practice to reflect larger geopolitical changes.[23] Indeed, as public historians in the United States seek to engage in work with partners from marginalized communities to explore and elevate their histories, the lessons learned from Museums Connect can guide them in negotiating and reducing power hierarchies. The greatest legacy of this ambitious transnational program is its ability to continue to inform public history practice in pushing against institutional and historic hierarchies of power on a local, regional, national, and international scale.

STATEMENT ON METHODOLOGY

A growing body of literature on community engagement and changing relationships between public historians and their publics not only informs the theoretical analysis of this book but also its research methodology. In the course of my work, I have considered my own subjectivity vis-à-vis the MHHE-BMCM projects, the Museums Connect program more broadly, and my colleagues and interviewees more specifically. In addition to grant documents, I relied on oral interviews with AAM and DOS officials as well as with Museums Connect and IPAM participants from all sides of the partnerships. In so doing, I have striven to assert the agency and perspectives of non-western individuals within a discipline that has deep historical roots in the colonization of non-western bodies.[1]

The power relations embedded in cross-cultural interviews are a central concern of my methodology. Many of the interviews were with non-English-speaking Museums Connect participants. Thus, in addition to carefully working to understand and navigate the power dynamics embedded in interviews conducted across ethnic, cultural, racial, and gender boundaries, I consulted the scholarship of a number of oral historians who work cross-linguistically. The limitations of my language skills prevented me from conducting interviews in any language other than English. I therefore asked narrators to describe rather than evaluate, given that some might feel inclined to respond in the affirmative for fear of seeming impolite or ungrateful.[2] It is possible that some of them, at both the U.S. and non-U.S. museums, felt obliged to "toe the party line"—that is, praise a program that provided their institutions with large sums of money—or paint their involvement in the best possible light. However, it is also possible that, as I am a British national, my narrators spoke more candidly about a U.S. program than they might have if I were from the United States. Regardless, I sought to explain to my narrators the nature of my academic study and emphasized that they should not view my research as a public relations exercise.[3] I also considered the narrators' experiences as a collective and used their stories and expressions to corroborate their individual interpretations. For example, the abundance of positive responses I received from all the respondents about the impact of the grants allowed me to surmise that their experience was generally very positive. However, I also interrogated the meaning of this collective tone to assess what it revealed about the project and the relationships that developed between the participants and their museums and a program that provided large amounts of funding for international travel and transnational work. To move past these rose-tinted recollections, I analyzed the interviews not just as sources of information but also as discursive tracts full of embedded meaning. Thus, I treated the words the narrators used as equal in importance to the stories they told.[4]

Many of the interviews took place via telephone or Skype so that I could gain the perspectives of participants across the globe. Two significant problems presented themselves during these interviews. The first related to building rapport with the narrators, which was much more difficult when we were not face to face and able to observe body language, facial expressions, and other nonverbal cues.[5] The second involved my concerns about potential misunderstandings based on the faulty assumption that words and phrases share the same meaning for native and non-native English speakers. To mitigate this problem, I shared this work with the narrators featured in this study to offer them a chance to suggest where I might have misunderstood their original words and meanings.[6] This step ensured that my analyses were read and considered by a multiplicity of stakeholders.[7] Drawing on Michael Frisch's concept of a shared authority and subsequent scholarship, I offered my narrators the opportunity to comment, with the proviso that the project was my own work and I maintained the right to make final interpretive decisions.[8] This back-and-forth with narrators enriched my analysis considerably.[9] For instance, upon receiving a draft of a chapter, one non-U.S. museum professional told me they felt that I had dismissed their interpretations of events in favor of those of the U.S. narrators who had reflected on the same project activities. Our spirited conversation gave me a much greater appreciation for the nuances of these moments under debate; and while we agreed to disagree about the ultimate interpretation, my analysis is richer and more nuanced for this discussion and reflection.

APPENDIX

Museums Connect Projects, 2008–2016

2008

DEAR MR. MANDELA, DEAR MS. PARKS

Michigan State University Museum, East Lansing, Michigan, USA
Nelson Mandela Museum, Mthatha, South Africa

INDO-U.S. SCIENCE CENTER DIVERSITY

New York Hall of Science, Queens, New York, USA
National Council of Science Museums, Kolkata, India
Science City, Bangalore, India

INSIDE/OUTSIDE/NORTH AND SOUTH

Museo de las Americas, Denver, Colorado, USA
Museo Nacional de Etnografia y Folklore, La Paz, Bolivia
Gallery "Casa del Caballero Águila," Puebla, Mexico

PROMOTING VOLUNTEERISM IN DUSHANBE

Black Pine Animal Sanctuary, Albion, Indiana, USA
Dushanbe Zoo, Dushanbe, Tajikistan

2009

CARRYING TRADITIONS ACROSS THE WATERS OF TIME: AINU AND PACIFIC NORTHWEST CULTURAL COLLABORATIONS

Burke Museum of Natural History and Culture, Seattle, Washington, USA
Ainu Association of Hokkaido, Sapporo, Japan

CREATING COMMUNITY COLLABORATION

Museum of History and Holocaust Education, Kennesaw, Georgia, USA
Ben M'sik Community Museum, Casablanca, Morocco

NOT JUST ANOTHER BRICK IN THE WALL: ENGAGING ITALIAN AND AMERICAN TEENS

Sci-Port: Louisiana's Science Center, Shreveport, Louisiana, USA
Parco Astronomico InfiniTo, Pino Torinese, Italy

WATER: USING THE COMMON TIE THAT BINDS

Roger Ehnstrom Nature Center, Wahpeton, North Dakota, USA
Bendery City Museum of Ethnography and Natural History, Bendery, Moldova

WE, THE PEOPLE: AFGHANISTAN, AMERICA, AND THE MINORITY IMPRINT

National Constitution Center, Philadelphia, Pennsylvania, USA
National Museum of Afghanistan, Kabul, Afghanistan

2010

BUILDING A TRANSATLANTIC BRIDGE

Westmoreland Museum of American Art, Greensburg, Pennsylvania, USA
LVR-Industriemuseum, Oberhausen, Germany

CONNECTING FINNISH AND ADIRONDACK COMMUNITIES

Wild Center, Tupper Lake, New York, USA
Heureka, the Finnish Science Centre, Vantaa, Finland

FROM THE ADIRONDACKS TO THE MIDDLE OF THE WORLD

World Awareness Children's Museum, Glens Falls, New York, USA
Museo de la Ciudad, Quito, Ecuador

INTERNATIONAL LEGACY YOUTH LEADERSHIP PROJECT

Birmingham Civil Rights Institute, Birmingham, Alabama, USA
Mandela House Museum, Soweto, South Africa
Apartheid Museum, Johannesburg, South Africa

IN THEIR OWN VOICES

Cincinnati Museum Center, Cincinnati, Ohio, USA
National Museums of Kenya, Lamu, Kenya

ISHARE: CONNECTING MUSEUMS AND COMMUNITIES EAST AND WEST

University of Colorado Museum of Natural History, Boulder, Colorado, USA
National Taiwan Museum, Taipei City, Taiwan

NAVIGATING DIFFERENCE: TRANSATLANTIC DIALOGUES ON IMMIGRATION

Ellis Island Immigration Museum, New York City, New York, USA
International Coalition of Sites of Conscience, New York City, New York, USA
Galata Maritime Museum, Genoa, Italy
Le Bois du Cazier, Charleroi, Belgium

SHARING BIODIVERSITY AND CULTURE

Discovery Museums, Acton, Massachusetts, USA
Tin Marin Children's Museum, San Salvador, El Salvador

YOUNG WOMEN SPEAKING THE ECONOMY

International Museum of Women, San Francisco, California, USA
Women's Museum in Denmark, Aarhus, Denmark
Ayala Museum, Makati City, Philippines
Sudanese Women's Museum, Omdurman, Sudan

2011

AT THE TABLE: CONNECTING CULTURE, CONVERSATION, AND SERVICE IN LATVIA AND THE UNITED STATES

National Constitution Center, Philadelphia, Pennsylvania, USA
National History Museum of Latvia, Riga, Latvia

COMMUNITY OF CONSERVATION: RESEARCH EXCHANGE EXPERIENCES FOR GLOBAL YOUTH

Lincoln Park Zoo, Chicago, Illinois, USA
National Museum of Niger Boubou Hama, Niamey, Niger

IDENTITIES: UNDERSTANDING ISLAM IN A CROSS-CULTURAL CONTEXT

Museum of History and Holocaust Education, Kennesaw, Georgia, USA
Ben M'sik Community Museum, Casablanca, Morocco

NOT JUST ANOTHER BUILDING ON THE STREET

Sci-Port Louisiana's Science Center, Shreveport, Louisiana, USA
Parco Astronomico InfiniTo, Pino Torinese, Italy

NUCLEAR WEAPONS TESTING LEGACY: THE TALE OF TWO CULTURES

National Atomic Testing Museum, Las Vegas, Nevada, USA
Karaganda Ecological Museum, Karaganda, Kazakhstan

RAINFOREST LEADERSHIP ACADEMY: CROSS-CULTURAL TEACHER TRAINING AND MENTORING

California Science Center, Los Angeles, California, USA
Maloka, Bogotá, Colombia

TWO MUSEUMS, TWO NATIONS, ONE IDENTITY

Art Museum of the Americas, Washington, DC, USA
Museo de Arte de El Salvador, San Salvador, El Salvador

WATCH YOUR WASTE E-MUSEUM

Arab American National Museum, Dearborn, Michigan, USA
Children's Museum Jordan, Amman, Jordan

2012

CORAL REEF AMBASSADORS

Birch Aquarium at Scripps College, La Jolla, California, USA
National Museum of Marine Biology and Aquarium, Checheng, Pingtung, Taiwan

DIGITAL SKIES STUDENT PARTNERSHIP

Chabot Space and Science Center, Oakland, California, USA
Hong Kong Space Museum, Hong Kong, China

GIRL AMBASSADORS FOR HUMAN RIGHTS

International Coalition of Sites of Conscience, New York City, New York, USA
Matilda Joslyn Gage Foundation, Fayetteville, New York, USA
Corporacion Parque por la Paz Villa Grimaldi, Santiago, Chile
Sri Lanka Plantation Workers' Museum, Paradeka, Sri Lanka

MUSLIM WOMEN'S ART AND VOICES

International Museum of Women, San Francisco, California, USA
Museum of Islamic Civilization, Sharjah, United Arab Emirates
Women's Museum in Denmark, Aarhus, Denmark
Ayala Museum, Manila, Philippines

NEXT STOP: BROOKLYN/DAKAR

Brooklyn Children's Museum, Brooklyn, New York, USA
ImagiNationAfrika, Dakar, Senegal

NORTH-SOUTH: ART AS A TOOL TO MEDIATE POLITICAL AND SOCIAL CONFLICT

Sonoma County Museum, Santa Rosa, California, USA
Gyeonggi Museum of Modern Art, Gyeonggi-Do, Republic of Korea

OBJECT STORIES EXCHANGE

Portland Art Museum, Portland, Oregon, USA
Museo Nacional de San Carlos, Mexico City, Mexico

P.A.U.S.E.: POLLINATORS/ART/URBAN AGRICULTURE/SOCIETY/AND THE ENVIRONMENT

Tohono Chul Park, Tucson, Arizona, USA
Saint Louis Zoo, St. Louis, Missouri, USA
National Museums of Kenya, Nairobi, Kenya

PAST TO PRESENT: U.S.-SINO BRIDGE OF CONNECTION

Pacific Aviation Museum Pearl Harbour, Honolulu, Hawaii, USA
Jianchuan Museum Cluster, Chengdu, Sichaun, China

WRITTEN IN ROCK: COLLABORATION AMONG AZERBAIJANI AND PUEBLO INDIAN COMMUNITIES

National Museum of the American Indian, Smithsonian Institution, Washington, DC, USA
Office of Policy and Analysis, Smithsonian Institution, Washington, DC, USA
Gobustan National Historical Artistic Preserve, Baku, Azerbaijan
In collaboration with the Indian Pueblo Cultural Center, Albuquerque, New Mexico, USA

2013

A JOURNEY THROUGH THE AFRICAN DIASPORA

Prince George's African American Museum and Cultural Center, North Brentwood, Maryland, USA
Museu Afro-Brasil, Sao Paulo, Brazil

ANCIENT SHORES, CHANGING TIDES—DEVELOPING LOCAL ARCHAEOLOGICAL HERITAGE EXPERTISE

Burke Museum of Natural History and Culture, Seattle, Washington, USA
Palawan State University Museum, Palawan, Philippines

DESIGN DIARIES INTERNATIONAL

Minnesota Historical Society, Saint Paul, Minnesota, USA
Palestinian Heritage Museum, Jerusalem

EMPOWER PARENTS: FOSTERING CROSS-CULTURAL NETWORKS BETWEEN FAMILIES WITH AUTISM

Queens Museum of Art, Queens, New York, USA
Museo ICO, Madrid, Spain

FLAG STORIES: CITIZENSHIP UNBOUND

SOMArts Cultural Center, San Francisco, California, USA
Islamic Art Museum of Malaysia, Kuala Lumpur, Malaysia

FOREST GUARDIANS

Three Mountain Alliance, Līhu'e, Hawaii, USA
Zoological Society of San Diego, San Diego, California, USA
Sicán National Museum, Ferreñafe, Peru

FROM THE GROUND UP: NUTRITIONAL VALUES AND CULTURAL CONNECTIONS

Phipps Conservatory and Botanical Gardens, Pittsburgh, Pennsylvania, USA
Gidan Makama Museum Kano, Kano, Nigeria

RETHINKING HOME: CLIMATE CHANGE IN NEW YORK AND SAMOA

American Museum of Natural History, New York City, New York, USA
Museum of Samoa, Apia, Samoa

SCALING THE WALLS/ESCALANDO PAREDES: CREATING URBAN GREEN SPACES

Children's Museum of Pittsburgh, Pittsburgh, Pennsylvania, USA
Interactive Science Museum, Quito, Ecuador

TURNING THE TABLE: UNDERSTANDING CROSS-CULTURAL MOVEMENTS

Guadalupe Cultural Arts Center, San Antonio, Texas, USA
Museo de Arte Contemporáneo Ateneo de Yucatán, Mérida, Mexico

2014

BY THE WORK OF HER HANDS: TEXTILE ARTS IN MOROCCO AND THE UNITED STATES

Fabric Workshop and Museum, Philadelphia, Pennsylvania, USA
Tangier American Legation Institute for Moroccan Studies, Tangier, Morocco

CITIZEN-LED URBAN ENVIRONMENTAL RESTORATION

Phillip and Patricia Frost Museum of Science, Miami, Florida, USA
Natural History Museum of Jamaica, Kingston, Jamaica

CITY OF PEACE: CHICAGO AND PHNOM PENH

Jane Addams Hull–House Museum, Chicago, Illinois, USA
Kraing Ta Chan Community Peace Learning Center, Kus Commune, Cambodia

COMMON GROUND: CONNECTING COMMUNITY THROUGH GARDENS

Monterey County Agricultural and Rural Life Museum, King City, California, USA
Casa K'inich Children's Museum, Copan, Honduras

COMMON NOTES: CONNECTING FOLK TRADITIONS THROUGH TECHNOLOGY

Clay Center for the Arts and Sciences of West Virginia, Charleston, West Virginia, USA
"Alexandru Stefulescu" Gorj County Museum, Târgu Jiu, Romania

CULTURAL REPERCUSSIONS OF CLIMATE CHANGE IN TWO COMMUNITIES: A TEENAGE VIEWPOINT

Academy of Natural Sciences of Drexel University, Philadelphia, Pennsylvania, USA
National Museum of Mongolia, Ulaanbaatar, Mongolia

DEFINING CULTURE IN POPULAR CULTURE

Pearl S. Buck House National Historic Landmark, Perkasie, Pennsylvania, USA
Pearl S. Buck Museum, Zhenjiang, China

E-MAMMAL INTERNATIONAL

North Carolina Museum of Natural Sciences, Raleigh, North Carolina, USA
Bombay Natural History Society, Mumbai, India
Museo de Paleontologia in Mexico, Guadalajara, Mexico

STORIES FROM THE HOME PLANET (HISTORIAS DE NUESTRO PLANETA)

James Ford Bell Museum of Natural History, University of Minnesota, St. Paul, Minnesota, USA
Corporación Parque Explora, Medellin, Colombia

2015

CONFRONT VIOLENCE THROUGH YOUTH-ORIENTED MEDIA

AS220, Providence, Rhode Island, USA
IZOLYATSIA, Kiev, Ukraine

CONNECTING COASTAL COMMUNITIES: AN INTERNATIONAL DIALOGUE ABOUT OCEAN CONSERVATION AND ECOTOURISM

Old Dartmouth Historical Society–New Bedford Whaling Museum, New Bedford, Massachusetts, USA
Húsavík Whale Museum, Húsavík, Iceland

DIALOGUES IN THE AFRICAN DIASPORA: YOUTH RECLAIMING COMMUNITY, IDENTITY, AND MEMORY

Caribbean Cultural Center African Diaspora Institute, New York City, New York, USA
National Museum Jamaica, Kingston, Jamaica

GIRLS DESIGN THE WORLD: SUPPORTING GREEN COMMUNITIES WITH STEAM

Minneapolis Institute of Arts, Minneapolis, Minnesota, USA
National Museums of Kenya, Nairobi, Kenya

HACKING SPACE: A STUDENT EXCHANGE TO SUSTAIN LIFE ON EARTH

Chabot Space and Science Center, Oakland, California, USA
Science City, West Bengal, India

YOUTH EMPOWERMENT THROUGH SOCIAL PRACTICE ART: STRATEGIES FOR COPING WITH VIOLENCE AND TRAUMA

Museum of Contemporary Art San Diego, La Jolla, California, USA
Museo Tamayo Arte Contemporaneo, Mexico City, Mexico

YOUTH MISSION TO MARS: EXPLORING SPACE TO ADDRESS SUSTAINABILITY ON EARTH

Space Center Houston, Houston, Texas, USA
Cité de l'Espace, Toulouse, France
Science Center, Singapore

2016

LIFELINES/ASPECTOS VITAIS: THE CONVEREGNCE OF ARTS, ECOLOGY, AND CULTURE IN THE AMAZON AND NEW ENGLAND

Stepping Stones Museum for Children, Norwalk, Connecticut, USA
Museu Paraense Emílio Goeldi, Belém, Brazil

MAYA FROM THE MARGINS: ARCHIVES AND EXPERIENCES OF HISTORY, IDENTITY, AND MIGRATION

Southern Historical Collection, University of North Carolina, Chapel Hill, North Carolina, USA
Archivo General de Estado de Yucatán, Mérida, Mexico

REEL STORIES

Arab American National Museum, Dearborn, Michigan, USA
Palestinian Heritage Museum, Jerusalem

WEAVING STRANDS OF KNOWLEDGE: CONNECTING CULTURE AND SCIENCE TO CLIMATE CHANGE

Montshire Museum of Science, Norwich, Vermont, USA
Folk Heritage Museum, Thimpu, Bhutan

WATERWAYS: CONNECTING COMMUNITIES

Museum Center at 5ive Points, Cleveland, Tennessee, USA
Museo de Bellas Artes de la Boca de Artistas Argentinos Benito Quinquela Martin, Buenos Aires, Argentina

YOUTH INNOVATIVE COMMUNITY SOLUTIONS

Intrepid Sea, Air, and Space Museum, New York City, New York, USA
Corporación Parque Explora, Medellín, Colombia

NOTES

INTRODUCTION

1. Thomas Cauvin, "The Rise of Public History: An International Perspective," *Historia Crítica* 68 (2018): 4.
2. For example, see Ana Maria Mauad, Juniele Rabêlo de Almeida, and Ricardo Santhiago, eds., *Histórica pública no Brasil: Sentidos e itinerários* (São Paulo: Letra e Voz, 2016); Paul Knevel, "Public History: The European Reception of an American Idea?," *Levend Erfgoed: Vakblad voor public folklore and public history* 6, no. 2 (2009): 4–8; Graeme Davison, "Public History," in *Oxford Companion to Australian History,* ed. Graeme Davison, John Hirst, and Stuart Macintyre (Melbourne: Oxford University Press, 1998), 532–35.
3 Serge Noiret and Thomas Cauvin, "Internationalizing Public History," in *The Oxford Handbook of Public History,* ed. James B. Gardner and Paula Hamilton (Oxford: Oxford University Press, 2017), 25.
4. Ibid., 26–27.
5. Jannelle Warren-Findley, "The Globalizing of Public History: A Personal Journey," *Public Historian* 20, no. 4. (1998): 11–20; Noiret and Cauvin, "Internationalizing Public History," 25–43; James B. Gardner and Paula Hamilton, "The Past and Future of Public History: Developments and Challenges," in Gardner and Hamilton, *The Oxford Handbook of Public History*, 8–9.
6. Gardner and Hamilton, "The Past and Future of Public History," 8–9.
7. International Federation for Public History–Fédération Internationale pour l'Histoire Publique, http://ifph.hypotheses.org.
8. International Coalition of Sites of Conscience, https://www.sitesofconscience.org.
9. William Willingham, "International Collaboration and Comparative Research," *Public History Commons,* June 22, 2015, http://ncph.org.
10. American Alliance of Museums, "Strategic Plan, 2016–2020," https://www.aam-us.org.
11. J. Michael Waller, "Introduction," in *The Public Diplomacy Reader,* ed. J. Michael Waller (Washington, DC: Institute of World Politics Press, 2007), 19; Richard T. Arndt, *The First Resort of Kings: American Cultural Diplomacy in the Twentieth Century* (Washington, DC: Potomac Books, 2005), xxi.

12. For reflections on the transnational turn, see Michael Kazin, "The Vogue of Transnationalism," *Raritan* 26, no. 3 (2007): 155–67; Ian Tyrrell, "Reflections on the Transnational Turn in United States History: Theory and Practice," *Journal of Global History* 4 (2009): 453–74; and Laura Briggs, Gladys McCormick, and J. T. Way, "Transnationalism: A Category of Analysis," *American Quarterly* 60, no. 3 (2008): 625–48.
13. Previous academic treatment of Museums Connect has focused on project reports or analyzing the program within the framework of globalization and the internationalization of the field. See, for instance, Jennifer W. Dickey, Samir El Azhar, and Catherine M. Lewis, "Introduction," in *Museums in a Global Context: National Identity, International Understanding,* ed. Jennifer W. Dickey, Samir El Azhar, and Catherine M. Lewis (Washington, DC: AAM Press, 2013), 12–13; and Jana Greenslit, "Museums Connect: The Next Chapter of International Collaboration" (master's thesis, University of Washington, 2015).
14. For an analysis of Museums Connect from the public diplomacy angle, see Natalia Grincheva, "Democracy for Export: Museums Connect Program as a Vehicle of American Cultural Diplomacy," *Curator* 58, no. 2 (2015): 146.
15. David Ledbetter, "BlogBack: AAM on Its State Department Collaboration," *Arts Journal,* July 17, 2007, https://www.artsjournal.com.
16. Arndt, *The First Resort of Kings;* U.S. Department of State, "Under Secretary for Public Diplomacy and Public Affairs," http://www.state.gov.
17. American Alliance of Museums, "Museums Connect: Building Global Communities," https://www.aam-us.org.
18. Tony Bennett, *The Birth of the Museum: History, Theory, Politics* (Abingdon, UK: Routledge, 1995).
19. Germain Bazin, "From the Museum Age," in *Museum Studies: An Anthology of Contexts,* ed. Bettina Messias Carbonell (Malden, MA: Blackwell, 2004), 20.
20. Edward P. Alexander and Mary Alexander, *Museums in Motion: An Introduction to the History and Function of Museums,* 2nd ed. (Plymouth, UK: AltaMira, 2007), 6–7. See also, Bennett, *The Birth of the Museum,* 21–27.
21. Bennett, *The Birth of the Museum,* 66; Robert W. Rydell, "World Fairs and Museums," in *A Companion to Museum Studies,* ed. Sharon Macdonald (Oxford: Wiley Blackwell, 2011), 135–51.
22. Duncan Cameron, "The Museum, a Temple or the Forum?," *Curator* 14, no. 1 (1971): 52.
23. "Metropolitan Art Museum," *New York Times,* May 26, 1872.
24. Warren Leon and Roy Rosenzweig, *History Museums in the United States: A Critical Assessment* (Champaign: University of Illinois Press, 1989), 7–12.
25. Alexander and Alexander, *Museums in Motion,* 7.
26. John Cotton Dana, "The Gloom of the Museum," in *Reinventing the Museum: The Evolving Conversation on the Paradigm Shift,* 2nd ed., ed. Gail Anderson (Lanham, MD: AltaMira, 2012), 33.
27. Catherine M. Lewis, *The Changing Face of Public History: The Chicago Historical Society and the Transformation of an American Museum* (Dekalb: University of Northern Illinois Press, 2005), 11–16; Jennifer W. Dickey, *A Tough Little Patch of History: "Gone with the Wind" and the Politics of Memory* (Fayetteville: University of Arkansas Press, 2014), 39–46.

28. Alexander and Alexander, *Museums in Motion,* 123; Richard Handler and Eric Gable, *The New History in an Old Museum: Creating the Past at Colonial Williamsburg* (Durham, NC: Duke University Press, 1997), 4; Jessie Swigger, *History Is Bunk: Assembling the Past at Henry Ford's Greenfield Village* (Amherst: University of Massachusetts Press, 2014), 2; Meringolo, *Museums, Monuments, and National Parks* (Amherst: University of Massachusetts Press, 2012), 55.
29. Jeffrey Trask, *Things American: Art Museums and Civic Culture in the Progressive Era* (Philadelphia: University of Pennsylvania Press, 2011), 234.
30. Lewis, *The Changing Face of Public History,* 3–10; Edward T. Linenthal and Tom Engelhardt, ed., *History Wars: The Enola Gay and Other Battles for the American Past* (New York: Holt, 1996), 1–8; Leon and Rosenzweig, *History Museums in the United States*, xviii; Linenthal and Engelhardt, *History Wars,* 5; Thomas F. Gieryn, "Balancing Acts: Science, Enola Gay, and History Wars at the Smithsonian," in *The Politics of Display: Museums, Science, Culture*, ed. Sharon Macdonald (New York: Routledge, 1998), 197–228.
31. Andrea A. Burns, *From Storefront to Monument: Tracing the Public History of the Black Museum Movement* (Amherst: University of Massachusetts Press, 2013), 2–4.
32. Amy Lonetree and Amanda J. Cobb, "Introduction," in *The National Museum of the American Indian: Critical Conversations,* ed. Amy Lonetree and Amanda J. Cobb (Lincoln: University of Nebraska Press, 2008), xviii.
33. Michael Frisch, *A Shared Authority: Essays on the Craft and Meaning of Oral and Public History* (Albany: State University of New York Press, 1990), xx.
34. Michael Frisch, "From *A Shared Authority* to the Digital Kitchen, and Back," in *Letting Go? Sharing Historical Authority in a User-Generated World,* ed. Bill Adair, Benjamin Filene, and Laura Koloski (Philadelphia: Pew Center for the Arts and Heritage, 2011).
35. Cameron, "The Museum, a Temple or the Forum?," 11–24; Bill Adair, Benjamin Filene, and Laura Koloski, eds., *Letting Go? Sharing Historical Authority in a User-Generated World* (Philadelphia: Pew Center for the Arts and Heritage, 2011); Gail Anderson, "Introduction: Reinventing the Museum," in Anderson, *Reinventing the Museum,* 1; Eilean Hooper-Greenhill, *Museums and the Shaping of Knowledge* (New York: Routledge, 1992), 1; Lisa C. Roberts, *From Knowledge to Narrative: Educators and the Changing Museum* (Washington, DC: Smithsonian Institution Press, 1997), 2–3.
36. Ivan Karp, "Introduction: Museums and Communities: The Politics of Public Culture," in *Museums and Communities: The Politics of Public Culture,* ed. Ivan Karp, Christine Mullen Kreamer, and Steven D. Lavine (Washington, DC: Smithsonian Institution, 1992), 7.
37. Katharine T. Corbett and Howard S. (Dick) Miller, "A Shared Inquiry into Shared Inquiry," *Public Historian* 28, no. 1 (2006): 15–38.
38. Ruth J. Abram, "Kitchen Conversations: Democracy in Action at the Lower East Side Tenement Museum," *Public Historian* 29, no. 1 (2007): 59–76; Maggie Russell-Ciardi, "The Museum as a Democracy-Building Institution: Reflection on the Shared Journeys Program at the Lower East Side Tenement Museum," *Public Historian* 30, no. 1 (2008): 40; Roberts, *From Knowledge to Narrative;* John H. Falk and Beverly K. Sheppard, *Thriving in the Knowledge*

Age: New Business Models for Museums and Other Cultural Institutions (Oxford: AltaMira, 2006)

39. See, for example, John Kuo Wei Tchen, "Creating a Dialogic Museum: The Chinatown History Museum Experiment," in Karp et al., *Museums and Communities: The Politics of Public Culture,* 320.
40. Corbett and Miller, "A Shared Inquiry into Shared Inquiry," 36–38.
41. Amy Lonetree, *Decolonizing Museums: Representing Native America in National and Tribal Museums* (Chapel Hill: University of North Carolina Press, 2012); Charlotte J. Macdonald, "Two Peoples, One Museum: Biculturalism and Visitor 'Experience' at Te Papa–'Our Place,' New Zealand's New National Museum," in *Contested Histories in Public Space: Memory, Race, and Nation*, ed. Daniel J. Walkowitz and Lisa Maya Knauer (Durham, NC: Duke University Press, 2009), 29–48; Ruth B. Phillips and Mark Salber Phillips, "Contesting Time, Place, and Nation in the First Peoples' Hall of the Canadian Museum of Civilization" in *Contested Histories in Public Space: Memory, Race, and Nation*, ed. Daniel J. Walkowitz and Lisa Maya Knauer (Durham, NC: Duke University Press, 2009), 49–70; David Neufeld, "Parks Canada, the Commemoration of Canada, and Northern Aboriginal Oral History," in *Oral History and Public Memories*, ed. Paula Hamilton and Linda Shopes (Philadelphia: Temple University Press, 2008), 7–30; Lonetree and Cobb-Greetham, *The National Museum of the American.*
42. See, for example, Cauvin, "The Rise of Public History"; Gardner and Hamilton, "The Past and Future of Public History"; and Noiret and Cauvin, "Internationalizing Public History."

CHAPTER 1: "STATE DEPARTMENT MUSEUMS"?

1. "State Department Funds World Museum Exhibits," *Morning Edition,* National Public Radio, July 17, 2007.
2. Ibid.
3. Lee Rosenbaum, "My NPR Soundbite," *Culturegrrl,* July 17, 2007, http://www.artsjournal.com.
4. Tony Bennett, *The Birth of the Museum: History, Theory, Politics* (Abingdon, UK: Routledge, 1995), 6.
5. Barbara Kirshenblatt-Gimblett, *Destination Culture: Tourism, Museums, and Heritage* (Berkeley: University of California Press, 1998).
6. Michael Frisch, *A Shared Authority: Essays on the Craft and Meaning of Oral and Public History* (Albany: State University of New York Press, 1990).
7. This approach to public history has not been universally embraced. National museums, for example, are still used to define a nation. See, for example, Robert C. Post, *Who Owns America's Past? The Smithsonian and the Problem of History* (Baltimore: Johns Hopkins University Press, 2013); and Alima Bucciantini, *Exhibiting Scotland: Objects, Identity, and the National Museum* (Amherst: University of Massachusetts Press, 2018).
8. Joseph S. Nye, Jr., *Soft Power: The Means to Success in World Politics* (New York: Public Affairs, 2004), x–xiii; Grincheva, "Democracy for Export: Museums Connect Program as a Vehicle of American Cultural Diplomacy," *Curator* (March 2015): 137–49.

9. Nye, *Soft Power,* 102–3.
10. Arndt, *The First Resort of Kings: American Cultural Diplomacy in the Twentieth Century* (Washington, DC: Potomac, 2005), 83–85.
11. Nye, *Soft Power,* x. Also see, for example, Frances Stonor Saunders, *The Cultural Cold War: The CIA and the World of Arts and Letters* (New York: New Press, 2001); and Nicholas J. Cull, *The Cold War and the United States Information Agency: American Propaganda and Public Diplomacy, 1945–1989* (Cambridge: Cambridge University Press, 2009).
12. Arndt, *The First Resort of Kings,* 157.
13. Saunders, *The Cultural Cold War,* 1–2.
14. Arndt, *The First Resort of Kings,* 146.
15. For a thorough discussion of these tours, see Penny M. Von Eschen, *Satchmo Blows Up the World: Jazz Ambassadors Play the Cold War* (Cambridge, MA: Harvard University Press, 2006).
16. Nye coined these phrases in *Soft Power,* 103.
17. "Public Law 402: The Smith-Mundt Act" (1948), in *The Public Diplomacy Reader,* ed. J. Michael Waller (Washington, DC: Institute of World Politics Press, 2007), 488.
18. Ibid.
19. Panel on International Information, Education, and Cultural Relations, *International Information, Education, and Cultural Relations: Recommendations for the Future* (Washington, DC: Center for Strategic and International Studies, 1975), 1.
20. Fulbright-Hays Act, H.R. 8666, P.L. 87–256 (1961), http://www2.ed.gov.
21. Mary Jeffers, "Expert Views on Public Diplomacy: The Next Four Years," *Take Five,* November 26, 2012, https://takefiveblog.org.
22. Arndt, *The First Resort of Kings,* xii.
23. U.S. Advisory Commission on Public Diplomacy, "1985 Report," in Waller, *The Public Diplomacy Reader,* 27.
24. Paul A. Smith, *On Political War* (Washington, DC: National Defense University Press, 1989), 7.
25. U.S. Advisory Committee on Cultural Diplomacy, "Cultural Diplomacy: The Linchpin of Public Diplomacy, April 15, 2005," in Waller, *The Public Diplomacy Reader,* 165–70.
26. Ibid., 169.
27. Nancy Snow, "International Exchanges and the U.S. Image," *Annals of the American Academy of Political and Social Science* 616, no. 1 (2008): 199.
28. John Lenczowski, "Keep the end purpose clear," in Waller, *The Public Diplomacy Reader,* 197.
29. Evan Ryan, statement at her nomination hearing before the Senate Foreign Relations Committee, 113th Cong., July 30, 2013.
30. Marta Filipová, ed., *Cultures of International Exhibitions, 1840–1940: Great Exhibitions in the Margins* (New York: Routledge, 2015); Robert W. Rydell, "World Fairs and Museums," in *A Companion to Museum Studies,* ed. Sharon Macdonald (Oxford: Wiley-Blackwell, 2011), 135–51.
31. Theodore Low, "What Is a Museum?," in *Reinventing the Museum: The Evolving Conversation on the Paradigm Shift,* 2nd ed., ed. Gail Anderson (Plymouth, UK: AltaMira, 2012), 45.
32. Ibid., 34.

33. Ibid., 365.
34. Arndt, *The First Resort of Kings,* 353–57.
35. Edward Steichen, curator, *The Family of Man* (New York: Museum of Modern Art, 1955); Arndt, *The First Resort of Kings,* 364–67, 370–71.
36. Michael L. Krenn, *Fall-Out Shelters for the Human Spirit: American Art and the Cold War* (Chapel Hill: University of North Carolina Press, 2005), 5–6.
37. Ran Zwigenberg, "'The Coming of a Second Sun': The 1956 *Atoms for Peace* Exhibit in Hiroshima and Japan's Embrace of Nuclear Power," *Asia-Pacific Journal* 10, no. 6 (2012): 1–16; Marilyn S. Kushner, "Exhibiting Art at the American National Exhibition in Moscow, 1959: Domestic Politics and Cultural Diplomacy," *Journal of Cold War Studies* 4, no. 1 (2002): 6–26.
38. Brian Wallis, "Selling Nations: International Exhibitions and Cultural Diplomacy," in *Museum Culture: Histories, Discourses, Spectacles,* ed. Daniel J. Sherman and Irit Rogoff (Minneapolis: University of Minnesota Press, 1994), 267.
39. Liam Kennedy, "Remembering September 11: Photography as Cultural Diplomacy," *International Affairs* 79, no. 2 (2003): 315–26. See also Sophie McIntyre, "The Art of Diplomacy: The Role of Exhibitions in the Development of Taiwan-China Relations," *Journal of Curatorial Studies* 4, no. 1 (2015): 56–77.
40. Wallis, "Selling Nations," 267; Daniel Walkowitz and Lisa Maya Knauer, "Introduction," in *Memory and the Impact of Political Transformation in Public Space,* ed. Daniel J. Walkwoitz and Lisa Mayer Knauer (Durham, NC: Duke University Press, 2004), 4; Anne Hennings, "The National Museum of China: Building Memory, Shaping History, Presenting Identity" (PhD diss., University of Heidelberg, 2013); Bucciantini, *Exhibiting Scotland.*
41. See, for example, Kushner, "Exhibiting Art at the American National Exhibition in Moscow, 1959," 6–26.
42. Heather Berry, personal communication, February 5, 2014.
43. Ibid.
44. Jennifer W. Dickey, Samir El Azhar, and Catherine M. Lewis, "Introduction," in *Museums in a Global Context: National Identity, International Understanding,* ed. Jennifer W. Dickey, Samir El Azhar, and Catherine M. Lewis (Washington, DC: American Alliance of Museums Press, 2013), 14.
45. Berry, personal communication.
46. Ron Theodore Robin, "Requiem for Public Diplomacy?," *American Quarterly* 57, no. 2 (2005): 347.
47. Mary Jeffers, personal communication, February 13, 2014.
48. U.S. Information Agency, "Options for Addressing Possible Budget Reductions," GAO/NSIAD-96-179 (Washington, DC, September 23, 1996), http://www.gpo.gov.
49. Arthur A. Bardos, "'Public Diplomacy': An Old Art, a New Profession," *Virginia Quarterly Review* (Summer 2001), http://www.vqronline.org.
50. William J. Clinton, "First Inaugural Address," January 20, 1993, *American Presidency Project,* http://www.presidency.ucsb.edu.
51. Walter Laqueur, "Save Public Diplomacy: Broadcasting America's Message Matters," *Foreign Affairs,* September 1, 1994, http://www.foreignaffairs.com.
52. USIA's budget peaked at $1.084 billion in 1992 before remaining stagnant throughout the rest of the decade. (It was funded at $1.099 billion in 1997.)

In 1999, the agency and its public diplomacy programs—with the goal of streamlining and reducing inefficiencies—were merged into DOS. See U.S. Information Agency, "Options for Addressing Possible Budget Reductions" (Chapter Report GAO/NSIAD-96-179), September 23, 1996, http://www.gpo.gov; and Kennon H. Nakamura, "U.S. Public Diplomacy: Background and Current Issues" (Congressional Research Service Report for Congress 7-5700, R40989), December 18, 2009, 14.

53. On the history of USIA and its decline, see, for example, Nicholas J. Cull, *The Cold War and the United States Information Agency: American Propaganda and Public Diplomacy, 1945–1989* (Cambridge: Cambridge University Press, 2009); and Nicholas J. Cull, *The Decline and Fall of the United States Information Agency: American Public Diplomacy, 1989–2001* (London: Palgrave MacMillan, 2012).
54. Laqueur, "Save Public Diplomacy."
55. George W. Bush, "President Bush Addresses the Nation," *Washington Post,* September 20, 2001.
56. Ibid.
57. Liam Kennedy and Scott Lucas, "Enduring Freedom: Public Diplomacy and U.S. Foreign Policy," *American Quarterly* 57, no. 2 (2005): 309. Also see Bardos, "Public Diplomacy"; Justin Hart, *Empire of Ideas: The Origins of Public Diplomacy and the Transformation of U.S. Foreign Policy* (Oxford: Oxford University Press, 2013); and Craig Hayden, *The Rhetoric of Soft Power: Public Diplomacy in Global Contexts* (Lanham, MD: Lexington, 2011).
58. U.S. Department of State, "Report of the Advisory Committee on Cultural Diplomacy" (Washington, DC, 2005), 1.
59. Arndt, *The First Resort of Kings,* xxi.
60. Ibid., 545.
61. U.S. Department of State, "International Affairs Function 150: Summary and Highlights" (2002–15), http://www.state.gov.
62. U.S. Department of State, "Preface to the FY2002 International Affairs (Function 150) Budget Request," http://www.state.gov.
63. James M. McCormick, "Introduction," in *The Domestic Sources of American Foreign Policy: Insights and Evidence,* ed. James M. McCormick (Plymouth, UK: Rowman and Littlefield, 2012), 3.
64. Richard G. Lugar, opening statement at the nomination hearings of Karen Hughes for under secretary of state, Senate Committee on Foreign Relations, 109th Cong., July 22, 2005.
65. Ibid.
66. Karen Lea Perez, personal communication, January 31, 2014.
67. French Regional and American Museum Exchange, https://framemuseums.org.
68. Karen Lea Perez, personal communication, April 14, 2014.
69. Ibid.
70. Berry, personal communication.
71. Mark Heppner, personal communication, June 5, 2015.
72. Kim Igoe, letter to Karen Lea Perez, July 12, 2006, American Alliance of Museums Archive, Washington, DC.
73. Berry, personal communication.

74. Perez, personal communication, January 31, 2014.
75. American Alliance of Museums, "Envisioning IPAM 2007–2009: Three Concepts for Collaboration," September 30, 2013, American Alliance of Museums Archive, Washington, DC.
76. Berry, personal communication.
77. Perez, personal communication, January 31, 2014.
78. Hishaam Aidi, "Leveraging Hip Hop in US Foreign Policy," *Al Jazeera*, November 7, 2011, http://www.aljazeera.com/.
79. Von Eschen, *Satchmo Blows Up the World.*
80. Hishaam Aidi, "Race, Rap, and Raison d'État," *Middle East Report* 260 (Fall 2011): 28.
81. Aidi, "Leveraging Hip Hop."
82. U.S. Department of State, "Report of the Advisory Committee on Cultural Diplomacy," 1.
83. Frisch, *A Shared Authority,* xx.

CHAPTER 2: "AFGHAN ON TOP AND AMERICAN ON BOTTOM"

1. Sayeh Hormozi, personal communication, January 21, 2015.
2. Jeffrey E. Stern, personal communication, August 28, 2015.
3. Bill Adair, Benjamin Filene, and Laura Koloski, "Introduction," in *Letting Go? Sharing Historical Authority in a User-Generated World,* ed. Bill Adair, Benjamin Filene, and Laura Koloski (Philadelphia: Pew Center for Arts and Heritage, 2011), 12.
4. See, for example, Elizabeth Edwards and Sigrid Lien, eds., *Uncertain Images: Museums and the Work of Photographs* (New York: Routledge, 2014); Serge Noiret, "Digital Public History Narratives with Photographs," *Public History Weekly,* October 22, 2015, https://public-history-weekly.degruyter.com; and Meg Foster, "Online and Plugged In? Public History and Historians in the Digital Age," *Public History Review* 21 (2014): 1–19.
5. National Museum of Afghanistan and National Constitution Center, implementation agreement, 1, courtesy of Hugh Allen.
6. Michael S. Sherry, "Patriotic Orthodoxy and American Decline," in *History Wars: The Enola Gay and Other Battles for the American Past,* ed. Edward Linenthal and Tom Engelhardt (New York: Holt, 1996), 99.
7. *National Constitution Center,* http://constitutioncenter.org.
8. "Best U.S. Schools—Constitution High School," *U.S. News and World Report,* n.d., https://www.usnews.com; *Constitution High School,* http://webgui.phila.k12.pa.us. The National Association of Museum Schools was created in 2014 to serve more than thirty such schools in the United States; see https://www.museumschools.org.
9. Hugh Allen, personal communication, January 9, 2015.
10. Stern, personal communication.
11. *Marefat High School,* https://marefat.wordpress.com.
12. Aziz Royesh, "Civic Education for Democracy in Afghanistan: Insights from the Kabul-Based Marefat High School," *National Endowment for Democracy,* March 15, 2012, http://www.ned.org.

13. *Marefat High School.*
14. Phillip Reeves, "From Afghanistan's Rubble, a Teacher Builds a School of Ideas," *Weekend Edition,* March 15, 2015, http://www.npr.org.
15. Stern, personal communication.
16. NMA and NCC, implementation agreement, 5; Stern, personal communication; Allen, personal communication.
17. NMA and NCC, implementation agreement, 15.
18. Allen, personal communication.
19. Adair et al., "Introduction," 12; Stern, personal communication; Jeffrey E. Stern, *The Last Thousand: One School's Promise in a Nation at War* (New York: St. Martin's, 2016).
20. Azizullah Royesh, personal communication, September 21, 2015.
21. Stern, personal communication.
22. Nasim Fekrat, personal communication, August 14, 2015.
23. Phil Zabriskie, "Hazaras: Afghanistan's Outsiders," *National Geographic* (February 2008), http://ngm.nationalgeographic.com.
24. Fekrat, personal communication.
25. Royesh, personal communication, September 21, 2015.
26. Hormozi, personal communication.
27. Azizullah Royesh, personal communication, September 22, 2015.
28. Adair et al., "Introduction," 13.
29. Nancy Hatch Dupree, "Cultural Heritage and National Identity in Afghanistan," *Third World Quarterly* 23, no. 5 (2002): 982–83; William C. S. Remsen and Laura A. Tedesco, "US Cultural Diplomacy, Cultural Heritage Preservation, and Development at the National Museum of Afghanistan in Kabul," in *Museums, Heritage, and International Development*, ed. Paul Basu and Wayne Modest (New York: Routledge, 2015), 137; Dana Visalli, "Afghanistan: The Legacy of British Empire. A Brief History," *Global Research*, March 22, 2013, http://www.globalresearch.ca; *National Museum of Afghanistan*, http://www.nationalmuseum.af; Dupree, "Cultural Heritage and National Identity," 982.
30. See, for example, Alima Bucciantini, *Exhibiting Scotland: Objects, Identity, and the National Museum* (Amherst: University of Massachusetts Press, 2018), 4–6; and Cristina Lleras, "National Museums, National Narratives, and Identity Politics," in *The Oxford Handbook of Public History*, ed. James B. Gardner and Paula Hamilton (Oxford: Oxford University Press, 2017), 349–68.
31. Omara Khan Massoudi, "The National Museum of Afghanistan," in *Afghanistan: Hidden Treasures from the National Museum, Kabul,* ed. Fredrik Hiebert and Pierre Cambon (Washington, DC: National Geographic Society, 2008), 35; *National Museum of Afghanistan.*
32. Dupree, "Cultural Heritage and National Identity," 983; Ann Dupree, Louis Dupree, and A. A. Motamedi, *A Guide to the Kabul Museum: The National Museum of Afghanistan* (Kabul: Afghan Tourist Organization, 1968).
33. Shaila Bhatti, *Translating Museums: A Counterhistory of South Asian Museology* (Walnut Creek, CA: Left Coast Press, 2012), 20.
34. Dupree, "Cultural Heritage and National Identity," 983.
35. Parin Dossa, *Afghanistan Remembers: Gendered Narrations of Violence and Culinary Practices* (Toronto: University of Toronto Press, 2014), 8.

36. Juliette van Krieken-Pieters, "Dilemmas in the Cultural Heritage Field: The Afghan Case and the Lessons for the Future," in *Art and Archaeology of Afghanistan: Its Fall and Survival*, ed. Juliette van Krieken-Pieters (Leiden: Brill, 2006), 201; Massoudi, "The National Museum of Afghanistan," 35–39.
37. Dupree, "Cultural Heritage and National Identity," 985; Massoudi, "The National Museum of Afghanistan," 37. See also Nancy Hatch Dupree, "Museum under Siege," *Archaeology* (March–April 1998), http://archive.archaeology.org; Nancy Hatch Dupree, "Museum under Siege: The Plunder Continues," *Archaeology* (May–June 1998), http://archive.archaeology.org; Dupree, "Cultural Heritage and National Identity," 986; Massoudi, "The National Museum of Afghanistan," 39; and Constance Wyndham, "Reconstructing Afghan Identity: Nation-Building, International Relations, and the Safeguarding of Afghanistan's Buddhist Heritage," in Basu and Modest, *Museums, Heritage, and International Development*, 159–63.
38. Ratish Nanda, "The Cultural Heritage of Afghanistan," *India International Center Quarterly* 30, no. 2 (2003): 101.
39. Massoudi, "The National Museum of Afghanistan," 37–38; and see, for example, Barbara Crossette, "U.N., in Shift, Moves to Save Art for Afghans," *New York Times*, March 31, 2001; National Endowment of Humanities, "Humanities Endowment Announces Afghanistan Initiative, Hosts President Karzai's First Official Visit to U.S. Museum," press release, May 23, 2005, http://www.neh.gov; and Alistair Lawson, "Afghan Gold: How the Country's Heritage Was Saved," *BBC News*, March 1, 2011, http://www.bbc.com.
40. Massoudi, "The National Museum of Afghanistan," 41; Fredrik Hiebert, "Curator's Preface," in Hiebert and Cambon, *Afghanistan*, 23; Remsen and Tedesco, "US Cultural Diplomacy, Cultural Heritage Preservation, and Development," 145.
41. Remsen and Tedesco, "US Cultural Diplomacy, Cultural Heritage Preservation, and Development," 137, 141–42.
42. Ibid., 108.
43. Kevin Sieff, "In Afghanistan, a New Approach to Teaching History: Leave Out the Wars," *Washington Post*, February 4, 2012; Remsen and Tedesco, "US Cultural Diplomacy, Cultural Heritage Preservation, and Development," 151; Fekrat, personal communication; "Azam," personal communication, September 16, 2015.
44. Wyndham, "Reconstructing Afghan Identity," 162–63.
45. Remsen and Tedesco, "US Cultural Diplomacy, Cultural Heritage Preservation, and Development," 141–42. On international traveling exhibitions, see also Daniel J. Walkowitz and Lisa Mayer Knauer, "Introduction," in *Memory and the Impact of Political Transformation in Public Space*, ed. Daniel J. Walkowitz and Lisa Mayer Knauer (Durham, NC: Duke University Press, 2004), 4; and Bucciantini, *Exhibiting Scotland*, 4–6.
46. Omar Sultan, "Introduction," in Hiebert and Cambon, *Afghanistan*, 30.
47. Hamid Karzai, "Foreword from the President of Afghanistan," in ibid., 13; Alma Freeman, "In Conversation with Afghan Museum Director Omara Khan Massoudi," *Asia*, January 23, 2013, http://asiafoundation.org.
48. Allen, personal communication; Omara Khan Massoudi, personal communication, trans. Zalmai Attarpoor and Fahim Rahimi, February 6, 2016.

49. Bruce Ackerman, *We the People: Transformations* (Cambridge, MA: Belknap Press of Harvard University Press, 2000), 2:3–4. The constitution of Afghanistan was ratified on January 26, 2004; a copy is available at http://www.afghanembassy.com.
50. *Being We the People*, digital exhibition, *National Constitution Center*, http://beingwe.constitutioncenter.org/; Stern, personal communication; "Main Exhibition," *National Constitution Center*, http://constitutioncenter.org.
51. Lauren Cristella, personal communication, September 23, 2015.
52. Ibid.
53. Ibid; "Constitution High School," *Civic Learning*, August 26, 2009, http://civiclearning.blogspot.com.
54. Stern, personal communication.
55. "Constitution High School," *Public School Review*, https://www.publicschoolreview.com.
56. Allen, personal communication.
57. Hormozi, personal communication.
58. Allen, personal communication.
59. "Samantha," personal communication, February 5, 2016; "Kayla," personal communication, February 11, 2016.
60. "Samantha," personal communication, February 9, 2016.
61. *Being We the People.*
62. Fekrat, personal communication.
63. Royesh, personal communication, September 21, 2015.
64. "Azam," personal communication.
65. Royesh, personal communication, September 21, 2015.
66. Fekrat, personal communication.
67. "Azam," personal communication.
68. "Samantha," personal communication, February 5, 2016.
69. Cristella, personal communication.
70. Jeffrey E. Stern and Hugh Allen, "Final Report: Collaborations Abroad, *Being We the People* Project," July 23, 2010, 9, courtesy of Hugh Allen; Stern, personal communication; Hormozi, personal communication; Cristella, personal communication.
71. Allen, personal communication; Stern, personal communication.
72. Allen, personal communication; Stern, personal communication.
73. Cristella, personal communication.
74. "Samantha," personal communication February 5, 2016; Allen, personal communication; Amanda L. Snyder, "Peace Offering," *South Philly Review*, May 20, 2010, http://www.southphillyreview.com.
75. "H.S. Students Exchanging Images with Counterparts in Afghanistan," WHYY, March 15, 2010, https://whyy.org; Royesh, personal communication, September 21, 2015; Fekrat, personal communication.
76. Allen, personal communication; Stern, personal communication.
77. Stern and Allen, "Final Report," 12.
78. Stern, personal communication; Stern and Allen, "Final Report," 12–13; Allen, personal communication.
79. Stern and Allen, "Final Report," 12–13; Allen, personal communication.
80. Royesh, personal communication, September 21, 2015.

81. "Azam," personal communication.
82. Tony Bennett, *The Birth of the Museum: History, Theory, Politics* (Abingdon, UK: Routledge, 1995), 20–21; Remsen and Tedesco, "US Cultural Diplomacy, Cultural Heritage Preservation, and Development," 150. In fact, the 1968 catalogue of the museum includes some items of Hazara dress as exhibited in the "Ethnographic Room"; see Dupree et al., *A Guide to the Kabul Museum*, 86–87.
83. "Azam," personal communication; Royesh, personal communication, September 21, 2015.
84. Stern, personal communication.
85. Stern and Allen, "Final Report," 13.
86. "Azam," personal communication.
87. Massoudi, personal communication.
88. Royesh, personal communication, September 22, 2015.
89. Massoudi, personal communication.
90. Hormozi, personal communication; Stern, personal communication.
91. *Being We the People*; Cristella, personal communication; Stern, personal communication; Hormozi, personal communication; Allen, personal communication.
92. Alex Irwin, "We the People: Afghanistan, America & the Minority Imprint @ the National Constitution Center," *Uwishunu*, June 2, 2010, http://www.uwishunu.com
93. Fekrat, personal communication.
94. Stern and Allen, "Final Report," 1.
95. Cristella, personal communication; Hormozi, personal communication; "Samantha," personal communication, February 5, 2016.
96. Jon Hurdle, "Exhibit Reveals Common Threads in Philadelphia, Kabul," *Reuters*, May 15, 2010, http://www.reuters.com. See also Snyder, "Peace Offering."
97. Adair et al., "Introduction," 13.
98. Stern, personal communication; Hormozi, personal communication; Allen, personal communication; Royesh, personal communication, September 21, 2015.
99. Cristella, personal communication.

CHAPTER 3: BEYOND AN "IMPERIALIST UNDERTAKING"?

1. One of the required readings for both project teams was Beverly Serrell, *Exhibit Labels: An Interpretive Approach* (Lanham, MD.: AltaMira, 1996).
2. See, for example, Robert R. Weyeneth and Daniel J. Vivian, "Public History Pedagogy: Charting the Course. Challenges in Public History Education, Guidance for Developing Strong Public History Programs," *Public Historian* 38, no. 3 (2016): 25–49; Alicia Ebbitt McGill, "Examining the Pedagogy of Community-Based Heritage Work through an International Public History Field Experience," *Public Historian* 40, no. 1 (2018): 54–83; and Na Li and Martha A. Sandweiss, "Teaching Public History: A Cross-Cultural Experiment. The First Public History Faculty Training Program in China," *Public Historian* 38, no. 3 (2016): 78–100.

3. Samir El Azhar, "Preface," in *Ben M'sik Community Museum: Building Bridges*, ed. Samir El Azhar (Casablanca: Force Equipment, 2012), 9.
4. Museum of History and Holocaust Education and Ben M'sik Community Museum, grant proposal: *Creating Community Collaborations* (2008), 2, Museum of History and Holocaust Education archive.
5. MHHE and BMCM, grant proposal: *Creating Community Collaborations,* 3; Catherine M. Lewis, personal communication, October 24, 2013; MHHE and BMCM, grant proposal: *Creating Community Collaborations,* 3. MHHE and BMCM were offered the unique opportunity to apply for a second Museums Connect grant because additional funding had become available after AAM and DOS made their selections for the 2010 grant cycle.
6. Edward Linenthal, *Preserving Memory: The Struggle to Create America's Holocaust Museum* (New York: Columbia University Press, 2001), 1; Georgia Commission on the Holocaust, https://holocaust.georgia.gov; Breman Museum, http://www.thebreman.org; MHHE and BMCM, grant proposal: *Creating Community Collaborations,* 2. For a full exploration of this evolution and historiography, see Linenthal, *Preserving Memory*, 5–16; Alison Landsberg, *Prosthetic Memory: The Transformation of American Remembrance in the Age of Mass Culture* (New York: Columbia University Press, 2004), 111–40; and, importantly, Peter Novick, *The Holocaust in American Life* (Boston: Mariner, 2000).
7. Museum of History and Holocaust Education, http://historymuseum.kennesaw.edu.
8. MHHE and BMCM, grant proposal: *Creating Community Collaborations,* 2.
9. Katharine T. Corbett and Howard S. Miller, "A Shared Inquiry into Shared Inquiry," *Public Historian* 28, no. 1 (2006): 15–38.
10. MHHE and BMCM, grant proposal: *Creating Community Collaborations,* 1; Corbett and Miller, "A Shared Inquiry into Shared Inquiry."
11. Museum of History and Holocaust Education and Ben M'sik Community Museum, grant proposal: *Identities: Understanding Islam in a Cross-Cultural Context* (2010), 6, Museum of History and Holocaust Education archive.
12. Mohamed Jadour, "The Attitudes of Some Moroccan Diplomats toward European Museums from 1786 to 1922," trans. Ahmad Ech-Charfi, in El Azhar, *Ben M'sik Community Museum,* 65–72.
13. Morocco was the first country to recognize U.S. independence in 1776; see U.S. Department of State, Office of the Historian, "Morocco," https://history.state.gov. This was mentioned to me with great pride more than once during my visit in December 2011.
14. Jadour, "The Attitudes of Some Moroccan Diplomats," 72.
15. Ibid.
16. Patrick Wolfe, "History and Imperialism: A Century of Theory, from Marx to Postcolonialism," *American Historical Review* 102, no. 2 (1997): 410. See also Edward Said, *Orientalism* (New York: Vintage, 1978).
17. Katarzyna Pieprzak, *Imagined Museums: Art and Modernity in Postcolonial Morocco* (Minneapolis: University of Minnesota Press, 2010), 5. See also Said, *Orientalism;* Homi Bhabha, *The Location of Culture* (New York: Routledge, 2004); Nicholas B. Dirks, ed., *Colonialism and Culture* (Ann Arbor:

University of Michigan Press, 1992); Frederick Cooper and Ann Laura Stoler, ed., *Tensions of Empire: Colonial Culture in a Bourgeois World* (Berkeley: University of California Press, 1997); and Pieprzak, *Imagined Museums*, 5–6.

18. Janet Abu-Lughod, *Rabat: Urban Apartheid in Morocco* (Princeton, NJ: Princeton University Press, 1980), xvii; Pieprzak, *Imagined Museums*, 8; Tony Bennett, *The Birth of the Museum: History, Theory, Politics* (Abingdon, UK: Routledge, 1995), 19.
19. Pieprzak and El Azhar are the two most prominent scholars of Moroccan museums writing in English. My language limitations unfortunately make me reliant on English-language scholarship, and I am grateful for their work. However, I acknowledge that their interpretations of museums in Morocco may not be representative of the whole.
20. Pieprzak, *Imagined Museums*, 8; Barbara Kirshenblatt-Gimblett, *Destination Culture: Tourism, Museums, and Heritage* (Berkeley: University of California Press, 1998), 132; Samir El Azhar, "The Ben M'sik Community Museum: Beyond Cultural Boundaries," in *Museums in a Global Context: National Identity, International Understanding*, ed. Jennifer W. Dickey, Samir El Azhar, and Catherine M. Lewis (Washington, DC: AAM Press, 2013), 26; Pieprzak, *Imagined Museums*, 3–4.
21. Today the thirteen national museums of Morocco are under the care of the National Foundation of Museums of Morocco. They include, among others, the Museum of History and Civilizations in Rabat, the Museum of Moroccan Arts in Tangiers, Mohammed VI Museum of Modern and Contemporary Art in Rabat, and the Dar Si Said Museum in Marrakesh.
22. Pieprzak, *Imagined Museums*, 4; Katarzyna Pieprzak, "Participation as Patrimony: The Ben M'Sik Community Museum and the Importance of the Small Museum in Morocco," in El Azhar, *Ben M'sik Community Museum*,12.
23. El Azhar, "The Ben M'sik Community Museum," 25.
24. Ibid., 29; Pieprzak, "Participation as Patrimony," 11. In contrast, see Bucciantini, *Exhibiting Scotland*, 1–9; and Cristina Llera, "National Museums, National Narratives, and Identity Politics," 352–53.
25. Meryem Saadi, "New Foundation Set to Renovate All Museums in Morocco," trans. Pascale Menassa, *Al-Monitor*, April 22, 2013, www.al-monitor.com; Pieprzak, *Imagined Museums*, 3.
26. El Azhar, "The Ben M'sik Community Museum," 25; Pieprzak, *Imagined Museums*, 68–69; Aomar Boum, "The Plastic Eye: The Politics of Jewish Representation in Moroccan Museums," *Ethnos* 74, no. 1 (2009): 53; Emanuela Trevisan Semi, "Museums of Moroccan Jews in Israel: What Kind of Memory?," in *Memory and Ethnicity: Ethnic Museums in Israel and the Diaspora*, ed. Emanuela Trevisan Semi, Dario Miccoli, and Tidor Parfitt (Newcastle upon Tyne, UK: Cambridge Scholars Publishing, 2013), 45–46. See also Michael Frank, "In Morocco, Exploring Remnants of Jewish History," *New York Times*, May 30, 2015.
27. MHHE and BMCM, grant proposal: *Creating Community Collaborations*, 3; Larry Hogue, letter to the editor, *Marietta Daily Journal*, September 14, 2011.
28. Julia Brock, Jennifer Dickey, Catherine M. Lewis, and Samir El Azhar, "Exploring Identities," *Public Historian* 34, no. 4 (2012): 19.
29. Robyn Gagne, "My Unexpected Journey: Forming Friendships across Cultural Boundaries," in El Azhar, *Ben M'sik Community Museum*, 61.

30. Brock et al., "Exploring Identities," 17; *Identities: Understanding Islam in a Cross-Cultural Context,* http://marb.kennesaw.edu.
31. Samir El Azhar, personal communication, October 15, 2013; El Azhar, "The Ben M'sik Community Museum," 37–39.
32. *Identities.*
33. The original grant proposal cited Lewis, *The Changing Face of Public History.*
34. Lewis, personal communication.
35. Jennifer W. Dickey, personal communication, October 30, 2013.
36. Members of the Subaltern Studies Group focus on intellectual colonialism and the inherent discursive imbalances when western intellectuals and academics attempt to provide a voice for subalterns by speaking for them or teaching them the language of western intellectuals. See, for example, the influential Gayatri Chakravorty Spivak, "Can the Subaltern Speak?," in *Marxism and the Interpretation of Culture,* ed. Cary Nelson and Lawrence Grossberg (London: Macmillan, 1988), 271–316. Ideas surrounding intellectual colonialism have also come up during other Museums Connect programs; see Elif M. Gokcigdem and Michelle M. Seaters, "One Zellij at a Time: Building Local and Global Cultural Connections and Creative Thinking Skills through an Exhibit of Islamic Arts for Children in Saudi Arabia," in Dickey et al., *Museums in a Global Context,* 168.
37. El Azhar, "The Ben M'sik Community Museum," 37.
38. Samir El Azhar, personal communication. October 15, 2013.
39. Lewis, personal communication.
40. El Azhar, personal communication.
41. Ibid.; El Azhar, "The Ben M'sik Community Museum," 36.
42. El Azhar, personal communication.
43. I participated in a number of exhibition workshops while in Morocco, including initial discussions of ideas that we wanted to feature in the exhibit, which Julia Brock and I led, and a session on exhibition concept statements, which Brock led. See *Identities.*
44. Ibid.
45. Brock et al., "Exploring Identities," 19; El Azhar, personal communication.
46. Brock et al., "Exploring Identities," 27.
47. Lewis, personal communication.
48. Ibid.; Dickey, personal communication, October 30, 2013; Jennifer Dickey, personal communication, August 17, 2015; Lewis, personal communication.
49. Dickey, personal communication, October 30, 2013; Samir El Azhar, personal communication, June 4, 2015.
50. Mary Jeffers, personal communication, January 31, 2014.
51. Samir El Azhar, personal communication, June 11, 2015; Samir El Azhar, "Conversation while Sipping Coffee," unpublished report, 1–3, Ben M'sik Community Museum archive; El Azhar, personal communication.
52. *Identities*; Ismail Chaki, personal communication to Julia Brock, April 2015.
53. Museum of History and Holocaust Education and Ben M'sik Community Museum, final report: *Creating Community Collaborations* (2011), 1, Museum of History and Holocaust Education archive.
54. Gagne, "My Unexpected Journey," 63; MHHE and BMCM, grant proposal: *Creating Community Collaborations,* 2.
55. Lewis, personal communication.

56. El Azhar, personal communication.
57. Elaine Sciolino, "Morocco Connection Is Emerging as Sleeper Threat in Terror War," *New York Times,* May 16, 2004; Andrea Elliot, "Where Boys Grow Up to Be Jihadis," *New York Times Magazine*, November 25, 2007; Jeffers, personal communication.
58. El Azhar, personal communication; Lewis, personal communication.
59. Michele Peregrin, "Museums and Communities Connect," *Dipnotes,* May 18, 2012, https://blogs.state.gov/stories.
60. Lewis, personal communication.
61. Dickey, personal communication.
62. El Azhar, personal communication, June 11, 2015.
63. Julia Brock, personal communication, October 28, 2013. These struggles are in keeping with the literature on community partnerships for museums that argue that building trust, rapport, and relationships is a long, time-intensive, and continuous process that is contested and politically charged. See, for example, the essays in Ivan Karp, Christine Mullen Kreamer, and Steven D. Lavine, eds., *Museums and Communities: The Politics of Public Culture* (Washington, DC: Smithsonian Institute, 1992); Dickey, personal communication.
64. Richard Harker, "Educating against 'Islamophobia': Creating an International Exhibit to Counter Intolerance," in El Azhar, *Ben M'sik Community Museum,* 44.

CHAPTER 4: ACTIVATING SITES OF CONSCIENCE

1. International Coalition of Sites of Conscience, https://www.sitesofconscience.org; Liz Ševčenko, "Public Histories for Human Rights: Sites of Conscience and the Guantánamo Public Memory Project," in *The Oxford Handbook of Public History,* ed. James B. Gardner and Paula Hamilton (Oxford: Oxford University Press, 2017), 141–62; Maggie Russell-Ciardi, "The Museum as a Democracy-Building Institution: Reflections on the Shared Journeys Program at the Lower East Side Tenement Museum," *Public Historian* 30, no. 1 (2008): 39–52.
2. Ahmad Ward, personal communication, November 14, 2013.
3. A number of historical sites wrestle with how to overcome great-man or -woman narratives. See, for example, Seth C. Bruggeman, *Here, George Washington Was Born: Memory, Material Culture, and the Public History of a National Monument* (Athens: University of Georgia Press, 2008); and Jennifer W. Dickey, *A Tough Little Patch of History: "Gone with the Wind" and the Politics of Memory* (Fayetteville: University of Arkansas Press, 2014).
4. Priscilla Cooper, personal communication, November 4, 2013; Laura Caldwell Anderson, personal communication, October 11, 2013.
5. Annie E. Combs, *History after Apartheid: Visual Culture and Public Memory in a Democratic South Africa* (Durham, NC: Duke University Press, 2003); Monica Eileen Patterson, "The Ethical Murk of Using Testimony in Oral Historical Research in South Africa," in *Oral History Off the Record: Toward an Ethnography of Practice,* ed. Anna Sheftel and Stacey Zembrycki (New York: Palgrave Macmillan, 2013), 201–18; Rafael Verbuyst, "History,

Historians, and the South African Truth and Reconciliation Commission," *New Contree* 66 (July 2013): 1–26.

6. Laura Anderson, personal communication.
7. Ibid.; Cooper, personal communication; Birmingham Civil Rights Institute, the Mandela House, and the Apartheid Museum, final report, undated, 464, Birmingham Civil Rights Institute archive.
8. Mandela House, http://www.mandelahouse.co.za; Apartheid Museum, http://www.apartheidmuseum.org; Anderson, personal communication; Cooper, personal communication. This trip was funded by money from a grant for BCRI's International Oral History Program.
9. On the way in which historic homes can become gendered shrines, see Bruggerman, *Here, George Washington Was Born;* Patricia West, *Domesticating History: The Political Origins of America's House Museums* (Washington, DC: Smithsonian Institution Press, 1999); and Roger C. Aden, *Upon the Ruins of Liberty: Slavery, the President's House at Independence Historical Park, Public Memory* (Philadelphia: Temple University Press, 2015).
10. Apartheid Museum; Mandela House; Birmingham Civil Rights Institute, http://www.bcri.org.
11. Anderson, personal communication; Laura Caldwell Anderson, "Promoting Civil and Human Rights Worldwide through Education: A Case Study of the Birmingham Civil Rights Institute," in *Museums in a Global Context: National Identity, International Understanding,* ed. Jennifer W. Dickey, Samir El Azhar, and Catherine M. Lewis (Washington, DC: AAM Press, 2013), 53; Ruwayda Davy, personal communication, August 5, 2015.
12. Anderson, personal communication; Jacqueline Nampi Masiza, personal communication, August 5, 2015.
13. Birmingham Civil Rights Institute, the Mandela House, and the Apartheid Museum, final proposal, undated, 4, Birmingham Civil Rights Institute archive.
14. For comparative studies of South Africa's and the U.S's history of racial apartheid and segregation, see George M. Fredrickson, *White Supremacy: A Comparative Study in American and South African History* (Oxford: Oxford University Press, 1981); and George M. Fredrickson, *Black Liberation: A Comparative History of Black Ideologies in the United States and South Africa* (Oxford: Oxford University Press, 1995).
15. In Apartheid South Africa each inhabitant of South Africa was required to be classified as "black", "white" or "coloured" by the 1950 Population Registration Act. "Indian" was later added as a further category of classification. Sean Field, "Imagining Communities: Memory, Loss, and Resilience in Post-Apartheid Cape Town," in *Oral History and Public Memory,* ed. Paula Hamilton and Linda Shopes (Philadelphia: Temple University Press, 2008), 107; Hillary John Deacon, "Heritage in African History," in *Toward New Histories for South Africa: On the Place of the Past in our Present,* ed. Shamil Jeppie (Landsowne, South Africa: Juta Gariep, 2004), 117–29; Shamil Jeppie, "Introduction: New History?," in ibid., 4; Leslie Witz, "Solly Sachs, the Great Trek, and Jan van Riebeeck: Settler Pasts and Racial Identities in the Garment Workers' Union, 1938–1952," in *Rethinking Settler Colonialism: History and Memory in Australia, Canada, Aotearoa New Zealand, and South Africa,* ed.

Annie E. Coombes (Manchester, UK: Manchester University Press, 2006), 24–44; Albert Grundlingh, "A Cultural Conundrum? Old Monuments and New Regimes: The Voortrekker Monument as Symbol of Afrikaner Power in a Postapartheid South Africa," in *Contested Histories in Public Space: Memory, Race, and Nation,* ed. Daniel J. Walkowitz and Lisa Maya Knauer (Durham, NC: Duke University Press, 2009), 159–60.

16. Grundlingh, "A Cultural Conundrum?" 158; Deacon, "Heritage in African History," 397.
17. Annie E. Coombes, "Introduction," in Coombes, *Rethinking Settler Colonialism,* 2; Andrew Hall and Cynthia Kros, "New Premises for Public History in South Africa," *Public Historian* 16, no. 2 (1994), 16; Annie E. Coombes, *History after Apartheid: Visual Culture and Public Memory in a Democratic South Africa* (Durham, NC: Duke University Press, 2003), 1. For a comprehensive history of the public histories of post-apartheid South Africa, see Coombes, *History after Apartheid.*
18. Crain Soudien, "Emerging Discourses around Identity in New South African Museum Exhibitions," in *Museum Studies: An Anthology of Contexts,* ed. Bettina Messias Carbonell, 2nd ed. (Hoboken, NJ: Wiley-Blackwell, 2012), 398; Coombes, *History after Apartheid,* 9. On the larger issues and challenges associated with expanding national histories to appeal to international tourists, see Leslie Witz, "Transforming Museums on Postapartheid Tourist Routes," in *Museum Frictions: Public Cultures/Global Transformations,* ed. Ivan Karp, Corinne A. Kratz, Lynn Szwaja, and Tomás Ybarra-Frausto (Durham, NC: Duke University Press, 2006), 107–34; Soudien, "Emerging Discourses around Identity," 400–402; and Coombes, *History after Apartheid,* 4.
19. Coombes, *History after Apartheid,* 14.
20. Ibid., 54–69.
21. Ibid., 118; International Coalition of Sites of Conscience; Ciraj Rassool, "Community Museums, Memory Politics, and Social Transformation in South Africa: Histories, Possibilities, and Limits," in Karp et al., *Museum Frictions,* 287–310; Field, "Imagining Communities," 108, 112.
22. Rassool, "Community Museums, Memory Politics, and Social Transformation," 288–95.
23. Coombes, *History after Apartheid,* 7–17. On the complexities that emerged from this conference, see Jeppie, *Toward New Histories for South Africa.*
24. Julia C. Wells, "In the Shadow of the Butcher: The Limits to Remembering in Post-Apartheid South Africa," *Public Historian* 36, no. 2 (2014): 57.
25. David Blight, *Race and Reunion: The Civil War in American Memory* (Cambridge, MA: Harvard University Press, 2001), 3–4.
26. Kevin Allen, "The Second Battle of Fort Sumter: The Debate over the Politics of Race and Historical Memory at the Opening of America's Civil War Centennial, 1961," *Public Historian* 33, no. 2 (2011): 94–109; Robert J. Cook, *Troubled Commemoration: The American Civil War Centennial, 1961–1965* (Baton Rouge: Louisiana State University Press, 2007).
27. Teresa S. Moyer and Paul A. Shackel, *A Devil, Two Rivers, and a Dream: The Making of Harpers Ferry National Historical Park* (Plymouth, UK: AltaMira Press, 2008), 151–74; W. Fitzhugh Brundage, *The Southern Past: A Clash of Race and Memory* (Cambridge, MA: Harvard University Press, 2008), 7.

28. Andrea A. Burns, *From Storefront to Monument: Tracing the Public History of the Black Museum Movement* (Amherst: University of Massachusetts Press, 2013), 3–4, 7–11, 185–86.
29. James Horton and Lois Horton, *Slavery and Public History: The Tough Stuff of American Memory* (Chapel Hill: University of North Carolina Press, 2008). See also Jill Ogline, "Creating Dissonance for the Visitor: The Heart of the Liberty Bell Controversy," *Public Historian* 26, no. 3 (2004): 49–58.
30. Leigh Raiford and Renee C. Romano, "Introduction: The Struggle over Memory," in *The Civil Rights Movement in American Memory,* ed. Renee C. Romano and Leigh Raiford (Athens: University of Georgia Press, 2006), xii; Jeff Levine, "How Far Have We Come? Civil Rights Museums Evolve and Transform," *Museum* (January–February 2015): 28, xii–xiv; Owen J. Dwyer, "Interpreting the Civil Rights Movement: Contradiction, Confirmation, and the Cultural Landscape," in Romano and Raiford, *The Civil Rights Movement in American Memory,* 15.
31. Public Law 96–428, October 10, 1980, http://govinfo.gov.
32. Anderson, "Promoting Civil and Human Rights Worldwide," 48.
33. Ibid., 49.
34. Birmingham Civil Rights Institute; Anderson, "Promoting Civil and Human Rights Worldwide," 49.
35. Fredrickson, *White Supremacy,* xi; Bobby M. Wilson, *America's Johannesburg: Industrialization and Racial Transformation in Birmingham* (Lanham, MD: Rowman and Littlefield, 2000), 1. A vast body of literature draws an explicit connection between South Africa and the American south. See, for example, Fredrickson, *Black Liberation;* and Robert Trent Vinson, *The Americans Are Coming! Dreams of African American Liberation in Segregationist South Africa* (Athens: Ohio University Press, 2012).
36. Birmingham Civil Rights Institute, Apartheid Museum, and Mandela House Museum, "The International Legacy Youth Leadership Project" brochure, Birmingham Civil Rights Institute archive; Anderson, "Promoting Civil and Human Rights Worldwide," 46.
37. BCRI, Apartheid Museum, and Mandela House, final proposal, 4, 20.
38. Ibid., 4–10.
39. BCRI, Apartheid Museum, and Mandela House, final report, 1.
40. Andrew Cedar, "Strengthening Relationships with South Africa's Young Leaders," *DipNote,* May 12, 2011, http://blogs.state.gov.
41. BCRI, Apartheid Museum, and Mandela House, final proposal, 4.
42. Davy, personal communication.
43. Ibid.; Masiza, personal communication.
44. "Miriam," personal communication, February 26, 2016.
45. "Lesedi," personal communication, February 13, 2016.
46. Barry McNealy, personal communication, October 12, 2015; Michelle Craig, personal communication, October 11, 2013; BCRI, Apartheid Museum, and Mandela House, final proposal, 4; "Michael," personal communication, February 2, 2016; John A. Brimley, "South African Students in Birmingham Celebrate Nelson Mandela International Day," *Birmingham News,* July 18, 2011.
47. BCRI, Apartheid Museum, and Mandela House, final proposal, 4; International Coalition of Sites of Conscience; Graham Black, "Embedding

Civic Engagement in Museums," in *Reinventing the Museum: The Evolving Conversation on the Paradigm Shift,* 2nd ed., ed. Gail Anderson (Plymouth, UK: AltaMira, 2012), 268.

48. Ward, personal communication; McNealy, personal communication.
49. Davy, personal communication; McNealy, personal communication.
50. BCRI, Apartheid Museum, and Mandela House, final report, 475; "Lesedi," personal communication.
51. Masiza, personal communication; Craig, personal communication; Anderson, personal communication. For examples of other contemporary museum programming that has sought to achieve these goals, see Abram, "Kitchen Conversations," 59–76.
52. Ward, personal communication.
53. Cooper, personal communication.
54. Anderson, personal communication.
55. Ibid.
56. McNealy, personal communication; Faith Karimi, "Nelson Mandela, Anti-Apartheid Icon and Father of Modern South Africa, Dies," *CNN,* December 6, 2013, http://www.cnn.com. See also "South Africa's Nelson Mandela dies in Johannesburg," *BBC,* December 6, 2013, http://www.bbc.com; "Nelson Mandela Dead at 95," CBC News, December 6, 2013, http://www.cbc.ca; and Leesha McKenny, "South Africa's 'Greatest Son,' Former President Nelson Mandela, Has Died at the Age of 95," *Sydney Morning Herald,* December 6, 2013, http://www.smh.com.au.
57. Brimley, "South African Students in Birmingham Celebrate Nelson Mandela International Day."
58. Ibid.; Anderson, "Promoting Civil and Human Rights Worldwide," 54.
59. Dwyer, "Interpreting the Civil Rights Movement," 18; McNealy, personal communication; Cooper, personal communication.
60. Dwyer, "Interpreting the Civil Rights Movement," 14–18. On the politics of commemoration and celebration versus a complex and nuanced interpretation, see John Bodnar, *Remaking America: Public Memory, Commemoration, and Patriotism in the Twentieth Century* (Princeton, NJ: Princeton University Press, 1993); and John R. Gillis, *Commemorations: The Politics of National Identity* (Princeton, NJ: Princeton University Press, 1996).
61. Mindy Duitz, "The Soul of a Museum: Commitment to Community at the Brooklyn Children's Museum," in *Museums and Communities: The Politics of Public Culture,* ed. Ivan Karp, Christine Mullen Kreamer, and Steven D. Lavine (Washington, DC: Smithsonian Institution, 1992), 242.
62. Masiza, personal communication; Yvette Chatman, personal communication, September 1, 2015.
63. Ward, personal communication.
64. Ibid.
65. Ibid.; Cooper, personal communication.
66. Craig, personal communication; Anderson, personal communication.
67. Masiza, personal communication.
68. Davy, personal communication; Masiza, personal communication.
69. Masiza, personal communication; Davy, personal communication.

70. Michele Peregrin, "Museums and Communities Connect," *DipNote,* May 18, 2012, https://blogs.state.gov.
71. Bill Adair, Benjamin Filene, and Laura Koloski, "Introduction," in *Letting Go? Sharing Historical Authority in a User-Generated World,* ed. Bill Adair, Benjamin Filene, and Laura Koloski (Philadelphia: Pew Center for the Arts and Heritage, 2011), 13.
72. Cooper, personal communication; Ward, personal communication; Anderson, personal communication.
73. Davy, personal communication; Masiza, personal communication.
74. Craig, personal communication; Anderson, "Promoting Civil and Human Rights Worldwide," 56.
75. Davy, personal communication; Masiza, personal communication; Anderson, personal communication; Craig, personal communication.

CONCLUSION

1. Bill Adair, Benjamin Filene, and Laura Koloski, "Introduction," in *Letting Go? Sharing Historical Authority in a User-Generated World,* ed. Bill Adair, Benjamin Filene, and Laura Koloski (Philadelphia: Pew Center for the Arts and Heritage, 2011), 11.
2. Na Li, "Going Public, Going Global: Teaching Public History through International Collaborations," *Public History Review* 22 (2015): 2.
3. International Coalition of Sites of Conscience, http://www.sitesofconscience.org.
4. Belinda Bozzoli, "Interviewing the Women of Phokeng," in *The Oral History Reader,* 2nd ed., ed. Robert Perks and Alistair Thomson (New York: Routledge, 1998), 155–65; Susan K. Burton, "Issues in Cross-Cultural Interviewing: Japanese Women in England," in ibid., 166–76.
5. Katherine T. Corbett and Howard S. Miller, "A Shared Inquiry into Shared Inquiry," *Public Historian* 28, no. 1 (2006): 36.
6. Tom Satwicz and Kris Morrissey, "Public Curation: From Trend to Research-Based Practice," in Adair et al., *Letting Go?,* 196.
7. Kathleen McLean, "Whose Questions, Whose Conversations?," in Adair et al., *Letting Go?,* 71.
8. Rebecca Conard, "Take-Away Thoughts: Reflecting on Four Case Studies," *Public History Review* 22 (2015): 74.
9. Nancy Fraser, "Rethinking the Public Sphere: A Contribution to the Critique of Actually Existing Democracy," *Social Text* 25/26 (1990): 63.
10. See, for example, Jana Greenslit, "Museums Connect: The Next Chapter of International Collaboration," master's thesis, University of Washington, 2015; and Natalia Grincheva, "Democracy for Export: Museums Connect Program as a Vehicle of American Cultural Diplomacy," *Curator* 58, no. 2 (2015): 137–50.
11. Fraser, "Rethinking the Public Sphere," 67.
12. Li, "Going Public, Going Global," 5.
13. Brooke Leonard, personal communication, April 11, 2019.
14. American Alliance of Museums, "*Museums Connect* Evaluation Findings," November 2017, 8–9, https://www.aam-us.org.

15. American Alliance of Museums, https://www.aam-us.org.
16. American Alliance of Museums, tweet, September 24, 2013, http://twitter.com.
17. Nina Simon, for example, questions the value of considering *what* counts at a museum rather than *who* ("Who Counts? Grappling with Attendance as Proxy for Impact," *Museum 2.0*, October 16, 2013, http://museumtwo.blogspot.com).
18. AAM, "*Museums Connect* Evaluation Findings."
19. Mindy Duitz, "The Soul of a Museum: Commitment to Community at the Brooklyn Children's Museum," in *Museums and Communities: The Politics of Public Culture*, ed. Ivan Karp, Christine Mullen Kreamer, and Steven D. Lavine (Washington, DC: Smithsonian Institution, 1992), 242.
20. John Kuo Wei Tchen's reflections on the Chinatown History Museum highlights the length of time and level of sustained, engaged interaction necessary for successful community engagement ("Creating a Dialogic Museum: The Chinatown History Museum Experiment," in Karp et al., *Museums and Communities*, 285–326).
21. Jennifer W. Dickey, personal communication, October 30, 2013; Laura Caldwell Anderson, personal communication, October 11, 2013.
22. Madeline Vadkerty, personal communication, June 3, 2015.
23. James B. Gardner and Paula Hamilton, "The Past and Future of Public History: Developments and Challenges," in *The Oxford Handbook of Public History*, ed. James B. Gardner and Paula Hamilton (Oxford: Oxford University Press, 2017), 8–9.

STATEMENT ON METHODOLOGY

1. See, for example, Patrick Wolfe, "History and Imperialism: A Century of Theory, from Marx to Postcolonialism," *American Historical Review* 102, no. 2 (1997): 388–420; Tony Bennett, *The Birth of the Museum: History, Theory, Politics* (London: Routledge, 1995); Barbara Kirshenblatt-Gimblett, *Destination Culture: Tourism, Museums, and Heritage* (Berkeley: University of California Press, 1998); and Annie E. Coombes, *Reinventing Africa: Museums, Material Culture, and Popular Imagination* (New Haven, CT: Yale University Press, 1994). See also Shaila Bhatti's study of Pakistan's public history, which seeks to move beyond the traditional positioning of western museology (*Translating Museums: A Counterhistory of South Asian Museology* [Walnut Creek, CA: Left Coast Press, 2012], 26).
2. Andrew F. Clark, "The Challenges of Cross-Cultural Oral History: Collecting and Presenting Pulaar Traditions on Slavery from Bundu, Senegambia (West Africa)," *Oral History Review* 20, nos. 1/2 (1992): 4–5.
3. Valerie Yow, *Recording Oral History: A Guide for the Humanities and Social Sciences*, 2nd ed. (Oxford: AltaMira, 2005), 205.
4. Alessandro Portelli, "What Makes Oral History Different," in *The Oral History Reader*, 2nd ed., ed. Robert Perks and Alistair Thomson (London: Routledge, 1998), 36.
5. According to Yow, when the interview begins, there must be "a period of listening and observing" (*Recording Oral History*, 96).

6. Saeeda Shah, "The Researcher/Interviewer in Intercultural Context: A Social Intruder!," *British Educational Research Journal* 30, no. 4 (2004): 561; Norton Wheeler, "Cross-Lingual Oral History Interviewing in China: Confronting the Methodological Challenges," *Oral History* 36, no. 1 (2008): 58–59.
7. Katherine Borland, "'That's Not What I Said': Interpretive Conflict in Oral Narrative Research," in Perks and Thomson, *The Oral History Reader,* 319.
8. Daniel Kerr, "'We Know What the Problem Is': Using Oral History to Develop a Collaborative Analysis of Homelessness from the Bottom Up," *Oral History Review* 30, no. 1 (2003): 27–45.
9. Borland, "'That's Not What I Said,'" 310–21.

INDEX